# Understanding Biblical Archaeology

## An Introductory Atlas

Paul H. Wright

cartaJerusalem

First published in 2014 by
**CARTA Jerusalem**

Copyright © 2014
Carta Jerusalem
18 Ha'uman Street, P.O.B. 2500,
Jerusalem 9102401, Israel
E-mail: carta@carta.co.il
www.carta-jerusalem.com

Cartography: Carta, Jerusalem

**Picture Sources**
Paul H. Wright: photographs on pages 4, 6, 7, 8, 12, 13, 15, 16, 19, 23, 24, 26, 27, 35, 36, 37, 41, 42, 45, 46
*The New Encyclopedia of Archaeological Excavations in the Holy Land*, The Israel Exploration Society and Carta, Jerusalem, 1993:
    photographs on pp. 10, 11, 21, 22, 29, 30, 32 (courtesy of E. Stern), 33 (top)
Ada Yardeni: pp. 14, 29, 33 (bottom), 39
Cairo, Egyptian Museum: p. 20 (top)
A. F. Rainey: p. 20 (bottom)
Ephraim Stern: p. 32
Reuben and Edith Hecht Museum, University of Haifa: p. 47
All other illustrations are from the archives of Carta Jerusalem

Great care has been taken to establish sources of illustrations. If inadvertently we failed to do so, due credit will be given
in the next edition.

All rights reserved. No part of this book may be reprinted or reproduced or utilized in any form or by any electronic, mechanical,
or other means now known or hereafter invented, including photocopying and recording, or in any information storage or retrieval
system, without prior permission in writing from the publisher.

ISBN: 978-965-220-846-0

Printed in Israel

# CONTENTS

What Is Biblical Archaeology?...........................................5

The Early Bronze (c. 3200–2300 B.C.) and Intermediate Bronze (c. 2300–2000 B.C.) Ages...............................10

The Middle Bronze Age (c. 2000–1550 B.C.)..................14

The Late Bronze Age (c. 1550–1200 B.C.) .....................18

Iron Age I (c. 1200–1000 B.C.) ........................................21

Iron Age II (c. 1000–586 B.C.) ........................................24

The Babylonian and Persian Periods (586–331 B.C.)......32

The Hellenistic (331–142 B.C.) and Hasmonean (142–63 B.C.) Periods .................................................35

The Early Roman (Herodian) Period (63 B.C.–A.D. 135) .40

Notes and References ....................................................48

# Maps & Plans

Main EB Sites in the Southern Levant ............................10

The Campaign of Pepi I, c. 2350 B.C..............................13

Main MB Sites in the Southern Levant ..........................14

Main LB Sites in the Southern Levant ...........................18

Tel Hazor—The Mound and Excavation Areas ..............19

Main Iron I Sites in the Southern Levant.......................21

Tell Qasile—Plan of the Iron I Temple Complex............23

Main Iron II Sites in the Southern Levant......................25

Tel Arad—Plan of the Citadel .........................................26

Tel Beer-sheba—Plan of the Iron II City........................28

Tel Megiddo—Plan of the Mound .................................28

'Ain Dara—Plan of the Temple ......................................30

Plan of Ahab's Palace in Samaria ..................................31

Main Sites of the Babylonian and Persian Periods in the Southern Levant.............................................32

Jerusalem in the Time of Nehemiah ..............................34

Main Hellenistic and Hasmonean Sites in the Southern Levant.............................................35

Plan of Hellenistic Mareshah/Marisa .............................36

Jerusalem in the Hasmonean Period ............................38

Main Early Roman (Herodian) Sites in the Southern Levant ......................................................40

Caesarea Maritima ........................................................41

Herodium—Plan of the Palace-Fortress ........................42

Plan of Masada..............................................................43

Jerusalem in the Second Temple Period .......................44

*(overleaf) A corner column with double Corinthian capital awaits excavation at Jerash, ancient Gerasa, in the highlands of Gilead. The column, once part of the courtyard of the temple of Artemis, stands* in situ. *Forty feet high, it is now nearly buried by the proverbial sands of time.*

**For Vivian and Vivienne—**
*A noble heritage has been entrusted to you.*
*Guard it well.*

# What is Biblical Archaeology?

Archaeology, generally defined, has to do with the recovery, study and interpretation of material remains from the past. Its basic tenet is that objects from the past provide a direct, though never unobstructed, window to the ways that people lived their lives prior to modern times. As such, archaeology is an important—indeed, a critical—tool for both the historian and the biblical scholar. But because the historian's primary focus is recovering the past through the witness of texts, the relationship between archaeology and history needs to be defined carefully. The discussion often becomes lively when the topic of the archaeologist or the historian is the world of the Bible, and even more so when the biblical scholar is also a theologian.

Over the years many of the people who have been interested in the archaeology of the southern Levant, whether they be professionals or laity, have been so precisely because of the land's connection with the Bible. Moreover, many of these folks are people who belong (or belonged) to faith traditions. This reality is a matter of pride to many, and chagrin to others. We don't have an historical record similar to the Bible from ancient Ammon, Moab, Edom or Philistia, nor do we have another document from classical or pre-classical antiquity that remains a sacred text for faith communities numbering over a billion people today.[1] This alone puts the Bible in a privileged position. All of this prompts interested scholars to interact with the issue of not only how archaeological and textual data from the ancient world should be integrated with each other, but how both might be related to matters of faith. Of all of the topics related to biblical archaeology, it is this that remains the most animated, and to a large extent defines what the discipline is, or might be, for scholars and laymen alike.

Scholars who consider archaeology to be an autonomous discipline, one that operates independently of biblical studies, prefer to use the term *Syro-Palestinian archaeology* when speaking or writing about the archaeology of the southern Levant. On the other hand, for those for whom archaeology is a sub-discipline of the eclectic field of biblical studies, the term *biblical archaeology* is a workable construct. A middle position has been suggested by Killebrew,[2] among others, who speaks of Syro-Palestinian archaeology in connection with work related to the broader geographical territory of the Levant and reserves the term biblical archaeology for more focused work related to the lands and time periods of the Bible itself. In the process of sorting out the issues, it is helpful to define biblical archaeology through a quick summary of its growth and development over the last century, then note its value for biblical studies in particular.

**The Growth and Development of Biblical Archaeology: Significant Players and Trends.** Archaeology is a relatively recent endeavor as far as formal inquiries into the past go, having begun in any meaningful way in the Middle East only in the latter half of the nineteenth century. Earlier explorers in the region such as Ulrich Seetzen (from 1802 to 1810), Johann Burckhardt (from 1808 to 1817), Titus Tobler (in 1835, 1845, 1857 and 1865) and Edward Robinson (in 1838 and 1852) pioneered methods of surface exploration and site identification, with Tobler and Robinson in particular interested in mapping the biblical record on the lands of Ottoman Palestine.[3] Yet actual digging only began somewhat later, in the 1860's with the work of Charles Wilson and Charles Warren in Jerusalem. They, too, were strongly motivated to recover the historic reality of the world of the Bible.

At about the same time, the archaeology of the ancient Near East gained great initial strides with the recovery of cuneiform and hieroglyphic languages in Mesopotamia and Egypt, respectively. Many of the excavated texts written in these scripts were religious in nature, and not a few included materials that seemed to parallel, or at least shed light on, the Bible. In 1890 the work of Flinders Petrie at Tell el-Ḥesi, a mound on the dry inland portion of the southern Philistine coastal plain, determined that changes over time to "insignificant trifles" such as pottery held the key to dating the sequence of earth layers that comprised mounds enclosing the remains of ancient cities (tells).[4] This provided archaeologists the first credible tool for dating ancient remains, and allowed them to associate bits of material culture with events known from historic records, including those of the Bible. As the nations of Europe prepared for the First World War, the effort to recover the world of the ancient Near East increased, partly to satisfy insatiable intellectual, scientific and religious appetites, partly to secure nationalistic rights to the Holy Land. Motives were certainly mixed, but throughout the early decades of the rise of archaeology explorers looking to invest the Bible with tangible realites from the past—and to one extent or another this was almost everyone in the day—had plenty of fodder on which to chew.[5]

*Edward Robinson, W. M. Flinders Petrie and William F. Albright (left to right), giants of the past in the field of biblical archaeology.*

Everything ratcheted up between the first and second world wars as, under the impetus of the American scholar William Foxwell Albright, biblical archaeology came into its own. Born to Methodist missionaries in Chile, Albright never lost the desire to integrate the latest discoveries in archaeology, philology and history with biblical studies. He was, for instance, the first to publish a comprehensive chronology of ancient Israel based on pottery typology, bringing a semblance of order to multiple efforts that had stemmed from Petrie's initial analysis. Though no stranger to historical criticism, Albright worked in reaction to the excesses of critical methodologies that were attacking the historical veracity of the Bible, believing that the so-called assured results of biblical criticism were anything but. A bevy of students, and then their students, followed in his wake. Throughout, the "Albright" or "biblical archaeology school" sought to find ways that archaeology could serve as an independent and supposedly neutral standard by which to verify the historicity—and theology—of biblical texts.[6]

At the same time, formal schools of archaeology were established in British Mandate Palestine: American, directed for many years by Albright himself, British, French and German. Each initially fulfilled an academic role that advocated biblical studies, though their institutional goals have certainly broadened in the decades since. They in turn had a clear influence on Israeli archaeology, which in the early days was very much interested in the biblical roots of the

*A clearly defined ash layer such as this one indicates the destruction of a site or part of a site. An ash layer includes vessels, here broken, which were in use at the time of the fire. By dating vessels found in sealed contexts, it is possible to build the chronology of an ancient site.*

modern state of Israel.[7] The archaeology of the southern Levant did not develop real scientific rigor until the advent of the Wheeler-Kenyon method in the 1950's. It was Sir Mortimer Wheeler and Dame Kathleen Kenyon who pioneered the method of excavating carefully measured and controlled squares separated by well-defined balks, thereby allowing archaeologists to pay close attention to the sequence of earth layers and material remains, especially pottery, associated with each. As a result, archaeologists gained the necessary tools to confidently gather and organize data that could be useful for identifying and dating remains at ancient sites.[8]

In the 1960's and 1970's archaeologists began to ask questions related to anthropology, ethnography and the social sciences generally, including the fields of environmental studies, cultural studies, social and economic studies, ethno-history and historical geography. The goal was to try to look at explanations of ancient processes that *seemed* to be more universal than those related to a specific written record, including (and for some archaeologists, *especially* including) the Bible. Such efforts prompted a diverse and inclusive study of the material remains of the past, which came to be known as the New Archaeology.[9] New Archaeology is as interested in micro-finds (seeds, pollen, fragments of bone or fibers and the like) as it is in museum pieces, and asks questions of the data that are strictly secular rather than being tied to a biblical studies approach that characterized much of the Albright years. As an example, archaeologists examine the chemical composition of potsherds to locate the source of the clay from which their pots were made, or analyze trace elements adhering to the pores of clay vessels in order to determine what products the vessels might have contained in antiquity. In doing so, they gain valuable data which can help historians reconstruct economic and social interactions of ancient people groups, including patterns of manufacture, trade and consumption.

For the large group of people who were interested in recovering the past *precisely because of* their interest in the Bible, archaeology lost some of its relevance in the wake of the more secular trends set by this New Archaeology. This coincided with a noticeable shift in biblical studies during the latter decades of the twentieth century toward literary, even ahistorical, interpretive approaches to the Bible which proceeded without regard to archaeological data. And in the mind of many, once the biblical text was gutted of its historical veracity (either through older schools of historical criticism, newer ones grounded in literary readings or any number of minimalist methodologies clamoring for attention at any given time), it remained gutted, a carcass to be stuffed instead with "the assured results of archaeology," contrary to the biblical record that they might be.[10]

At the same time, the influence of the Bible and especially the combined weight of an interested (and funding) public continues to set much of the agenda for

*Pottery analysis and restoration is an important part of the process that moves data from the field to publication.*

*The mound of Tel Qashish (Tell el-Qassis), perhaps biblical Helkath (Josh 19:25; 21:31), rises from the banks of the reedy Kishon River at the western end of the Jezreel Valley. Adjacent to fertile fields and a perennial source of water, this tel, with a classic trapezoid shape, is typical of many from Bronze Age Canaan. Sloped sides such as these often preserve a system of ramparts constructed to protect the residents who lived within the city walls up top.*

scholars working in the archaeology of the southern Levant.[11] In recent years there has been a return to methodologies that ask how archaeology might be able to reconstruct specific historical scenarios that are related to the biblical period, or even illumine or illustrate accounts of events recorded in the Bible itself.[12] The feeling that the Bible is, by any estimation, a privileged text, and that a scholar would be remiss if it were not used as a source of data for recovering the world of ancient Israel, has returned to the forefront of the discussion. Today biblical archaeology by any name is a vibrant field, with no lack of energy spent on uncovering data and placing it in contexts that are meaningful for the biblical scholar.

**Archaeology as a Tool for Recovering the Past.** Before asking how archaeology might help the student of biblical studies, we should first pause to first reflect on the value of archaeology as a tool for recovering the past. Dever notes several contributions that archaeology can make to the historian; each speaks of the relationship between material culture and texts.[13]

1. Archaeological data stands as an independent witness to historical realities described in ancient texts as well as to overall living conditions assumed by such texts.
2. Archaeological data comes out of the ground clean, unedited and unbiased, although as it is studied and analyzed it is certainly subject to interpretation (more on this later). Written documents such as literary or religious texts, or formal administrative documents found in archaeological excavations, were certainly edited as they were being composed in ancient times. It is *that* bias, rather than ours, that is the relevant point of study. In contrast, many other documents brought to light by excavations seem to have been the unedited jottings of scribes meant for mundane or everyday use. These include letters or bookkeeping notations specific to a situation at hand. Like texts of social media today, such texts often include variants of spelling or grammar, the creative use of words, and cultural insights that were more authentic to real speech or living situations than are those preserved by language found in formal or canonical writings intended by their authors or editors for posterity.
3. Archaeological data is *realia*, that is, objects or parts of objects that once actually existed, that were made by specific people for specific purposes and that were discarded (or destroyed) for specific reasons. In contrast, literary and religious texts speak of interpreted worlds where reality also has to be sought in situations that spurred the minds of their authors.
4. The amount of archaeological data available to scholars is always expanding. Unlike a text (especially a sacred text which is part of a canon), the full collection of archaeological material known to scholars at any given time is never a closed corpus. Rather, it is a potentially unlimited source of new and sometimes unfamiliar data that increases our awareness of the past with each new excavation.

The benefits of archaeology for those already familiar with ancient texts are obvious. But there are problems inherent to the data which

*The work of the archaeologist is never done. Here a workman restores the mosaic floor of the Byzantine church in Petra, Jordan. Sites such as this have been preserved for the visiting public, offering a very tangible way to interact with our shared heritage of the past.*

prompt several words of caution. First, it must be remembered that there is no archaeological record *per se* waiting to be dug out of the ground. Rather, what remains is the random preservation of scattered and fragmented materials from the past. Moreover, it is not possible for the archaeologist to predict with any degree of certainty what might be dug up. If the Bible is criticized for being "selective, ancient and theologically oriented," the archaeological record is composed of remains that are "scattered, random and incomplete."[14] A second caution is that for all its value as an independent, unedited witness to the past, archaeological objects do not come out of the ground with labels. To cite Anson Rainey:

> The main drawback of archaeological evidence is its *ambiguity*.... What goes into the record is the archaeologist's *opinion* of the meaning of the evidence,[15]

however well-reasoned and backed by available data it might be. Indeed, it is the continually expanding nature of archaeological data that makes scholarly interpretations almost always necessarily tentative and incomplete.

All of this prompts us to ask the question, What then is an archaeological "fact"? In the eyes of an awaiting public, an archaeological fact is not nearly as exciting as what might be expected. This is a broken pot. Here is a partially preserved wall. That is a destruction layer. While facts such as these have an objectivity of their own, they do not "speak" until they are incorporated into a larger body of data held together by a set of interpretive assumptions that make sense out of the disparate parts to the extent that it is possible to do so at any given moment. One might safely come to say that "this is a wheel-made cooking pot for wheat mash," "here is a domestic house characteristic of Israelites in Iron Age II," or "that is evidence of the Assyrian invasion of Philistia in the late eighth century B.C." But to further extrapolate from these interpreted facts axioms such that the diet of ancient Israelite villagers was primarily grain-based, that the biblical family was an economic and social institution that functioned relatively independently within the confines of a walled set of relatively egalitarian rooms, or that Sargon's advance through Philistia was checked by Assyria's need to maintain functioning local economic centers in the region in advance of their push across the Sinai to Egypt, is more risky, even though any or all of these conclusions might be on the right track. Rainey was right when he quipped, "archaeology is the science of digging a square hole and the art of spinning a yarn from it."[16] In the end, for all of the data at their disposal, archaeologists (and historians) do well to speak not of laws or of proofs but rather of various trajectories, probabilities or tendencies of evidence. In the end, the assured results of archaeology are often as debatable as the assured results of biblical criticism continue to be.

**The Value of Archaeology for Biblical Studies.** Does archaeology, then, have credible value for biblical studies? Very much so, in that by giving shape, color and shading to our picture of the world of the Bible, it fills in and sharpens our understanding of the context(s) in which the Bible was written and about which it speaks. On the most basic level, archaeology can provide samples of material objects used during the time of the Bible. But it often also uncovers objects that are actually mentioned in the Bible itself, be they common items such as lamps (Mt 25:1) or gates (Ruth 4:1) or things more specific such as the water tunnel Hezekiah's workmen hewed beneath Jerusalem (2 Kgs 20:20) or Peter's Capernaum home (Mk 1:29, if these identifications are indeed correct). And occasionally archaeological finds are quite personal, such as when the names of officials known from the Bible appear on clay seal impressions (*bullae*; e.g., Gemariah son of Shaphan the scribe; Jer 36:10).[17] In cases like this we can be quite sure that we have an object that a biblical personality actually touched. But even more significantly, archaeologists are also learning methodologies that allow them to extrapolate data from material objects by which they can make statements about the economic, social or religious forces that gave such objects their particular usefulness or form. Why the need for a gate or a seal impression in the first place, archaeologists are asking, and why make it of *that* material or in *this* particular style or shape? While in the end archaeology cannot determine what people in the ancient world might have *thought*, it can say something about what they *did*, and suggest something about the presence of cultural values or historical forces as a result. For example, archaeologists are currently investigating:

- the method and timing of the emergence of ancient Israel (as well as the origins of the Philistines, Moabites, Edomites, Ammonites, etc.) in the land of Canaan;
- how ancient Israel (and its neighbors) developed from tribal to village life, and then to statehood;
- what polytheism, monolatry (belief in one supreme deity without denying the existence of others) or monotheism might have implied in ancient Israel in practical terms;

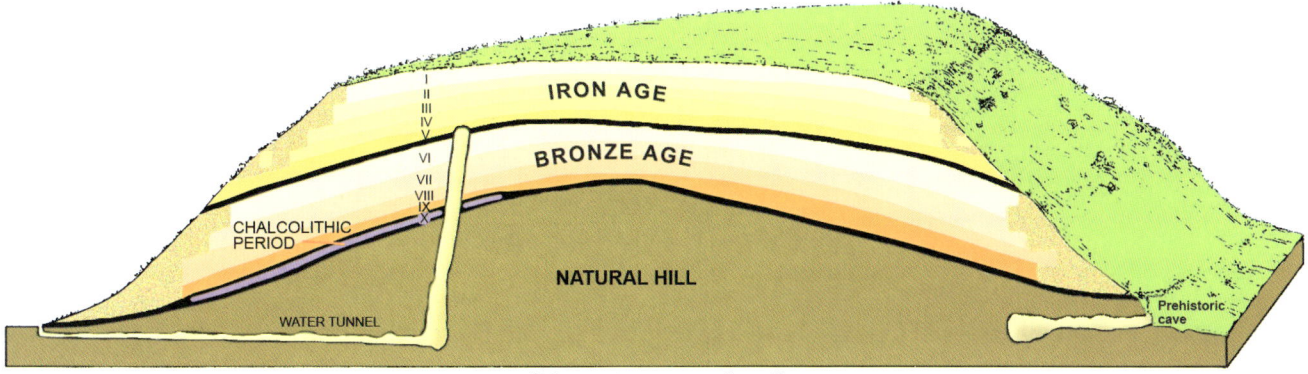
*Schematic section of a tell.*

- how and when ancient Israel's religious system became centralized in Jerusalem;
- ancient Israel's response to the empires that conquered the southern Levant (Egypt, Assyria, Babylon, Persia, Greece and Rome), and especially how Israel interacted with various cultural forces that settled in the area (e.g., Hellenism);
- the interaction between various regions of the southern Levant in any given time period, for example the interface between populations living west and east of the Jordan River during the Iron Age, or between people groups living in Galilee and those of Judea during the first century A.D.;
- what was distinctive about ancient Israel among its neighbors;
- how village life differed from urban life in ancient Israel; and
- the varieties of Judaism that existed in the ancient world during the first century A.D.

In addressing issues such as these, archaeology provides an incremental but significant growth in our ability to understand the basic fabric of life of the biblical world. In the process of doing so, it also helps scholars better illustrate, understand and assess the referents, images and claims of the Bible.

Archaeology also helps scholars recover the languages of the world of the Bible. Many inscriptions or jottings written in Hebrew as well as in cognate languages such as Moabite, Ammonite, Edomite and Aramaic, or in languages written in cuneiform and hieroglyphic scripts or in Greek or Latin, have seen the light of day thanks to the archaeologist's trowel.[18] Here the archaeologist works hand in hand with the epigrapher. Language, as a rule, offers a much better window into thought processes of an individual or a society than uninscribed material objects ever could.

With the study of texts (philology) comes inevitable questions about the identity and intent of an author (or authors), or of an editor (or editors) of the text. This in turn prompts a set of investigative processes used primarily by the historian, though with significant input by the archaeologist. For instance, does a biblical statement reflect the cultural values and norms of time period of the episode presented (e.g., the days of David and Solomon) or those of an author or editor who might be composing his work much later (e.g., the Chronicler who was active after the return from exile)? And so, by implication, does the Bible in any given instance reflect the material culture of the people mentioned in the text, or that of the author of the text? Or to what extent might it speak to both? In this regard the discussion between minimalists and maximalists (these terms apply equally well to those working with the text as those working with material culture) is particularly lively.[19]

By providing a credible context, the archaeologist can help the biblical scholar determine which interpretations of the Bible are most likely, or correct and sharpen interpretations that need correcting and sharpening.[20] This is the most justified use of the term *biblical archaeology*. For advocates of the historicity of the biblical record, an additional question is often asked: Can (or should) archaeology be used to prove or disprove one's faith, or even one's world view? The answer must be No. All attempts at integrating archaeological, textual and interpretative data aside, for believers, the Bible can stand on its own; for those who don't, it doesn't have to.

**A Note on Nomenclature.** Finally, a word on labels and terms. There is general scholarly agreement to divide the archaeological history of the southern Levant that relates to the Bible into the following time periods:
- The Early Bronze Age (3200–2000 B.C.)
- The Middle Bronze Age (2000–1550 B.C.)
- The Late Bronze Age (1550–1200 B.C.)
- The Iron Age (1200–586 B.C.)
- The Babylonian (or Exilic) Period (586–539 B.C.)
- The Persian Period (539–331 B.C.)
- The Hellenistic Period (331–142 B.C.)
- The Hasmonean Period (142–63 B.C.)
- The Early Roman (or Herodian) Period (63 B.C.–A.D. 132)

Several of these periods are typically further subdivided, giving us Early Bronze I, II, III and IV, Middle Bronze I and II, Late Bronze I and II, Iron Age I and II, and designating the Hasmonean Period as the final part of the Hellenistic Period. These in turn are divided even further as changes in material culture warrant (e.g., Iron IIA, B and C). The nomenclature is mixed, with the names of the earlier periods reflecting a now-outdated notion about the worldwide use metals and the latter periods named after peoples that assumed political control over the southern Levant. The earlier dates are general and typically reflect large scale changes in material culture or settlement patterns, while the latter dates are quite specific in that they reflect known historic changes in political control. Aharoni suggested changing the names of the metal ages to match the latter pattern, calling the Bronze Ages the Canaanite Period and the Iron Age the Israelite Period.[21] While there is logic behind his initiative, the idea never caught on, perhaps because it is specific to only a portion of the southern Levant.

An important question is, do these designated periods realistically reflect actual changes in material culture in the ancient world? The answer is sometimes yes, sometimes no, with a great deal of discussion in between. For instance, scholars typically combine Early Bronze IV with Middle Bronze I based on a similarity of material remains and call it the Intermediate Bronze Age. Similarly, the Late Bronze Age seems to have been a transitional period, at the same time preserving the remnants of the Middle Bronze Age while anticipating the forms of the Iron Age. As might be expected, defining the seams between the periods is a lively exercise. In any case, these archaeological periods will be the organizing structure for the following chapters.

# The Early Bronze (c. 3200–2300 B.C.) and Intermediate Bronze (c. 2300–2000 B.C.) Ages

**Basic Characteristics.** The Early Bronze Age (EB) saw the appearance of permanent settlements in the portions of the hill country, plains and valleys of the southern Levant where rainfall exceeds 15 inches per year. Altogether over 300 EB sites are known in the region. Ninety percent of these are found in areas which had not been settled during the Chalcolithic Age (4500–3500 B.C.), the archaeological period immediately prior when settlements, much smaller in scale, were found mostly in the arid regions of the land. Indeed, it was during EB that many of the sites that became

**MAIN EB SITES IN THE SOUTHERN LEVANT**

dominate throughout the biblical period had their first urban phase. These include Dan, Hazor, Beth-shean, Taanach, Megiddo, Gezer, Bethel, Jerusalem, Lachish, Jericho and Arad, as well as others with shorter overall life spans such as Beth Yerah, Jarmuth, Ai (et-Tell) and Tell el-Far'ah North (Tirzah). The EB strata are found, most naturally, at the deepest part of these tells.

The introduction of the donkey and the ox as domesticated beasts of burden allowed the people of the Early Bronze Age to engage in heavier and more efficient methods of cultivation, opening new lands to agriculture and allowing new products to be tilled. Olives and vines in particular were first widely grown in the area during the Early Bronze Age, with oil and wine becoming staples of export and trade. The Early Bronze Age also saw a significant increase in the cultivation of lentils and grains. This, with sheep and goat herding, became the standard economy of the Levant until modern times.

The Early Bronze Age was the first age of urbanization in the southern Levant. The establishment of towns and cities throughout EB was a gradual process, and not simultaneous in all regions of the land. It began with the rise of agricultural surpluses and trade in EB I (c. 3200–3000 B.C.), then reached maturity with the erection of fortifications and large public buildings in EB II and III (c. 3200–2300 B.C.). The best example of an urban city in the southern Levant during the third millennium B.C. is Arad. Arad grew from an unfortified settlement in EB I to a 25–acre city in EB II, fortified by a wall estimated to be 1200 meters (three-quarters of a mile) in length enclosing a basin-shaped area in which runoff rainwater, the water source of the city, collected in a single central reservoir. There is archaeological evidence of a number of smaller, unwalled settlements appearing in the vicinity of EB urban centers such as Arad, Megiddo, Beth-shean, Tell el-Far'ah North and Shechem, from which it is possible to posit patterns of economy in which urban, agricultural and pastoral (herding) elements coexisted. Still, the construction of fortifications in EB suggests not only a centralized authority at each urban center, but also intercity conflict. On the other hand, there is no clear evidence in the archaeological record of newcomers (i.e., invaders) of which the urban residents might have been afraid.

A summary of forms typical of the material culture of the Early Bronze Age follows:
- Urban centers that were fortified were usually surrounded by solid walls with projecting towers. The walls of Arad, Aphek, Ai (et-Tell), Jericho and Jarmuth were two to three meters wide, while those at Megiddo and Beth Yerah as well as the later EB phases at Ai, Jericho and Jarmuth were massive, up to seven to eight meters in width. The towers projecting from these walls were often rectangular, though those at Arad, Jericho and Ai were apsidal, with the short, outermost wall of the tower curved or apse-shaped. City gates were relatively simple in construction, usually just a gap in the wall flanked by towers.
- The earliest EB houses had mud brick walls on field stone foundations. In the more mature EB phases even houses found

*Clay box in the shape of a broad room, EB II, from Arad. This is likely a model of a temple or house.* (NEAEHL)

*EB II storage jar from Arad. (NEAEHL)*

*Typical Khirbet Kerak Ware, EB III, found at Afula. (NEAEHL)*

*EB cultic stela engraved with a stick figure depicting the god Dumuzi, from Arad. (NEAEHL)*

in valleys which largely lacked stones, such as Arad, had stone superstructures. Early Bronze houses were typically broad room in shape (rectangular with the entrance on one of the longer sides), with a single room as the dwelling unit.
- Early Bronze Age temples were also typically broad rooms, such as those found at Arad, Ai and Megiddo. The roofs were supported by interior columns placed on stone pillar bases. At Megiddo three identical broad room temples were found adjacent to a large round, raised open air stone platform.
- Water for domesticated use was stored in runoff reservoirs at the lowest point of towns (Ai, Arad and Jarmuth), since more sophisticated systems for collection and distribution had not yet been developed.
- Pottery in the Early Bronze Age was mostly hand made, though the wheel was used to make certain parts such as the vessel base. Wavy ledge handles rather than rounded loop handles typical to later periods were common. The decoration of EB vessels shows widespread use of red slip and burnish, offering some of the most beautiful pottery ever made in the southern Levant. Characteristic vessels are Abydos ware, very fine vessels for scented oils, medicines and cosmetics, and Khirbet Kerak (= Beth Yeraḥ) ware, thick and not as well made but highly burnished with red upper exterior surfaces and black below.
- There is relatively poor attestation of metals throughout the Early Bronze Age most of which were copper (the use of bronze for tools and implements would not become common until the Middle Bronze Age).
- There is also poor attestation of objects of art, though a few seals and seal impressions are known. The most notable EB object of art is the incised "dying and rising" stela from Arad that depicts the god Dumuzi as a stick figure representing the seasonal cycle of grain agriculture.

An overall increase in population density within the urban sites throughout the Early Bronze Age is assumed from an increase in the number of structures found during the period, though actual numbers of people are impossible to determine. A fair population estimate for Arad suggests two to three thousand inhabitants during its most prosperous days, with a total population estimate for all urban areas of the southern Levant of approximately 150,000 persons. The overall population of the land was certainly more, on the assumption that most people lived in small settlements or tent communities that are not easily archaeologically recoverable. Differences in the quality of recoverable vessels suggests that the standard of living in the smaller villages was somewhat less than that of persons living in the larger centralized urban areas, as might be expected on sociological grounds. Though the number of urban sites declined from EB II to EB III (Arad, for instance, completely disappeared between EB II and the Iron Age), those that survived into EB III (e.g., Beth Yeraḥ, Megiddo, Ai, Jarmuth, Jericho, Dan, Beth-shean and Lachish) reached the height of prosperity. This may suggest an overall movement toward centralization of the economy throughout the period. In the end these patterns set the economic and political standard for city-state settlement in the southern Levant for the next two millennia.

The processes of urbanization in the southern Levant during the Early Bronze Age followed by a few centuries the rise of the first age of urbanization in Mesopotamia and Egypt. This was a necessary frontier land for Egypt, its closest international neighbor, and there is clear archaeological evidence (primarily in the form of imported pottery vessels) of an Egyptian presence in the Negev basin and along the coastal plain as early as EB I. The name of the very first king of united Egypt, Narmer, was found incised on potsherds in EB I contexts at Arad, Tel ʽErani, Tel Malḥata, Tel Ḥalif and at Lod. Narmer set the stage for Egyptian economic interests in the area, a pattern that would continue throughout all ages of antiquity (Egyptian political dominance of the southern Levant would come a millennium later in the Late Bronze Age). While Egyptian interests in southwest Asia are fairly well documented even from written records from Egypt, there is a total lack of indigenous written records from the southern Levant in the Early Bronze Age. We don't know what the EB residents of what would become Canaan called themselves, or what they called their homeland (the name Canaan doesn't appear until the second millennium B.C.). An Egyptian text from the Intermediate Period (2300–2000 B.C.), popularly called "The Autobiography of Weni", speaks of an Egyptian invasion of the coastal areas of the southern Levant during the days of the Egyptian king Pepi I. This text gives us the only contemporary name for the place, and it is likely a pejorative:

*The Early Bronze city of Arad was situated within a large, shallow basin in the eastern part of the Negev. The wall of the city traced the perimeter of the basin. A large pit at the lowest point of the middle of the site collected rainfall for use throughout the year. Broad room structures have been uncovered in every area of EB Arad that has been excavated.*

*A small group of explorers stand in the Early Bronze gate of Jarmuth at the end of a long day in the field. The massive walls of the gate are two meters (over six feet) wide.*

> This [Egyptian] army returned in safety,
> After it had hacked up the land of the Sand-Dwellers...²²

Unlike the end of later periods, there is no evidence of a unified, consistent destruction of sites that brought about the end of the Early Bronze Age. Rather, there was an irregular though overall decline in the number of settled sites from EB II to EB III, then a gradual decline into the Intermediate Bronze Age when urbanization in the southern Levant disappeared entirely. The process seems to have begun in the south (perhaps the invasion of Egypt under Pepi I played a role), then spread to the north. Overall conditions suggest local periods of unrest throughout the third millennium B.C.; Jericho, for instance, experienced six phases of building and destruction throughout the Early Bronze Age. Archaeologists differ in their explanations of the overall cause—was it warfare, general unrest, a weakening of international trade or climate change?²³—but the timing of the disappearance of urbanization in the southern Levant is concurrent with the collapse of urban civilizations in Mesopotamia (the kingdom of Akkad) and Egypt (the Old Kingdom or Age of the Pyramids).

The Intermediate Bronze (IB) Age in the southern Levant was exactly that, a period of approximately three centuries characterized by unwalled settlements, scattered structures and poor material culture in which the local economy was basically one of small scale, seasonal agriculture, sheep and goat herding, and hunting. Foreign

## THE CAMPAIGN OF PEPI I, C. 2350 B.C.

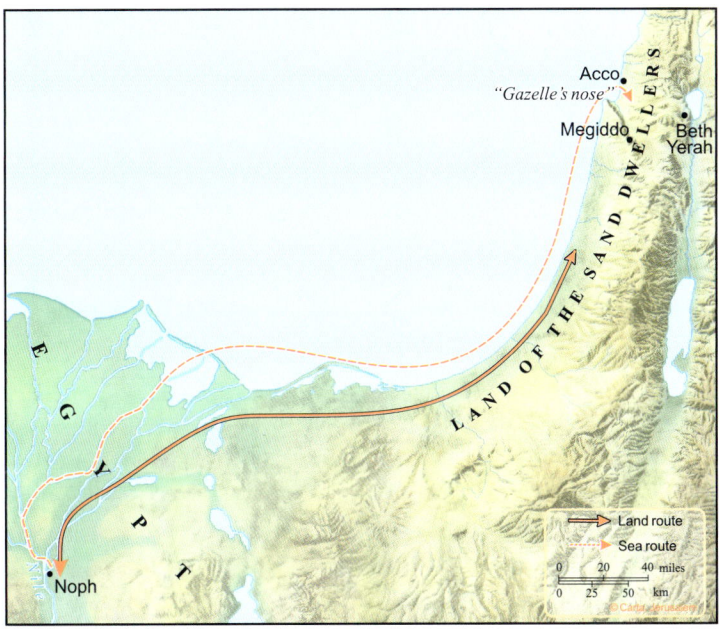

trade connections were essentially lacking, as is evidence of unified political structures. The population of the area was probably one-tenth that of EB II and EB III. These were the bare remnants of EB urban culture, and archaeologists debate whether the people living in the land represent new populations who moved in, indigenous peoples who had to resort to survivalist lifestyles, or peoples who had been on the fringes of the EB culture all along.[24] Some IB sites were built on the abandoned mounds of EB settlement (e.g., Hazor, Megiddo, Beth-shean and Jericho), but most are found at new locations. Intermediate Bronze Age peoples in the hill country often lived in caves, while those in the valleys and plains typically constructed broad room structures made of mud brick.

The settlements that are most characteristic of the period are the many small sites in the arid regions of the south (the Negev and Negev highlands). These are typically round structures (two to four meters in diameter) with a single stone pillar supporting a roof composed of radial beams covered by flat stones, together with adjacent round stone pens for animal husbandry. Many shaft-tomb cemeteries have been found in the hill country (tombs will survive long after surface structures disappear), and on the Golan Heights archaeologists have studied large dolmens which served to mark IB burials. The pottery of IB is generally rough and crudely made, largely without use of the wheel, and when decorated done so with incisions or poorly painted red or white stripes. Surprisingly there is an increase in the use of metal (bronze) for tools and weapons. For some archaeologists the material culture of IB represents remnants of Early Bronze, prompting the designation EB IV; for others it better anticipates the start of a renewed period of urbanization, hence the name MB I. "Intermediate Bronze Age" has come to be a reasonable compromise,[25] reflecting terminology similar to the contemporary Intermediate Period in Egypt.

**Biblical Connections.** Chronologically the Early and Intermediate Bronze Ages are prior to the biblical period but included here because they set context. As noted, the overall patterns of economy, especially the type of crops and livestock raised, are typical of those seen in the Bible (cf. Deut 8:8). The symbiotic relationship between urban centers, dependent villages and area herders is as well. The EB period also sets the initial pattern for the phenomenon of the city-state, an economic and political organization which would come into its fore as the Canaanite social structure that Israel faced upon entering the land at the end of the Late Bronze Age. Moreover, although the indigenous populations of the southern Levant have left us with no written documents at all, it was during this time in Mesopotamia and Egypt that epic and religious texts that find parallels in the biblical account began to take their classic forms (e.g., the stories of Creation and the Flood).

There is an overall awareness in the Bible's earliest stories of indigenous peoples who had inhabited the southern Levant since the earliest of times. While the archaeological evidence suggests that there was a discontinuity of population in the southern Levant between the Early and Middle Bronze Ages, it is possible that the memory of hoary antiquity found in the Bible has roots in the cultures of the third millennium B.C.. The Rephaim in particular seem to be recognized by the biblical authors as belonging to a once-powerful culture of Transjordan which had already essentially disappeared before Israel arrived in the land (Gen 14:5; Deut 2:10–11, 20; 3:11–13; Josh 12:4). Place names, too, reflect the same sense of a much older set of indigenous populations (e.g., Ai, lit. "the ruin," appropriately remembered today as the EB city at et-Tell, "the mound," was largely a ruin in the days of Joshua). If the patriarchs are to be placed in the Middle Bronze Age, then at least some of the peoples already in the land when they arrived (Gen 15:19) may have had roots in the Early or Intermediate Bronze Ages.

*Dolmens such as this marked burials on the Golan in the Intermediate Bronze Age. Over thirty have been excavated; many more are known from surveys. The semi-nomadic populations responsible for burying their dead in graves underneath the dolmens left no trace of either houses or settlements used by the living.*

# The Middle Bronze Age (c. 2000–1550 B.C.)

**Basic Characteristics.** The Middle Bronze Age (MB) is characterized by a revival of urban culture in the southern Levant. This apparently arose out of pockets of urban life that had persisted throughout the Intermediate Bronze Age in north Syria and along the northern Mediterranean (Phoenician) coast. The transition between EB and MB is very clear in the archaeological record, perhaps the most obvious distinction between any two periods in the ancient history of the southern Levant. The data suggests to archaeologists that a new set of populations settled in the region with the rise of the Middle Bronze Age.[26] A gradual change in the material culture within the MB has led archaeologists to subdivide the period into MB IIA (c. 2000–1750 B.C.) and MB IIB (c. 1750–1550 B.C.; recall that MB I has been renamed the Intermediate Bronze Age).

## MAIN MB SITES IN THE SOUTHERN LEVANT

The first half of the second millennium B.C. was also a true international age in the history of Mesopotamia and Egypt. A number of written documents from Egypt's Middle Kingdom (=MB IIA) and Second Intermediate / Hyksos Period (=MB IIB), from the Old Babylonian and Old Assyrian Empires in Mesopotamia, and from north Aramean kingdoms such as Mari on the Middle Euphrates provide an overall historical narrative into which the archaeological data of the southern Levant can be set. Perhaps most importantly, such documents provide synchronisms which can be used to establish pegs for dating archaeological remains in the region. For instance, cylinder seals in the style of Hammurabi found in tombs at Jericho firmly date settlement there to the mid-eighteenth century B.C. (according to the generally accepted Middle Chronology which dates Hammurabi to 1792–1750 B.C.). The Egyptian Execration Texts[27] which date to the nineteenth and eighteenth centuries B.C. mention places such as Laish (Dan), Hazor, Acco, Megiddo, Shechem, Aphek, Ashkelon, Lod and Jerusalem as worthy of Egyptian punitive attention. In doing so, they give witness to a network of strong city-states in what was becoming the land of Canaan during MB IIA. Mention of Laish and Hazor in the Mari texts of Zimri-Lim, a contemporary of Hammurabi, show that both cities were on the international tin-trade route in the eighteenth century.[28] A number of rather sophisticated cuneiform texts, including literary, lexical and mathematical texts have been found at in MB IIB and LB strata in excavated sites along the international highway in the southern Levant (Ashkelon, Aphek, Megiddo, Hazor). Together these show that even though Egypt was the closer international power, Akkadian was the trade language of the day.[29] By them we can posit the existence of schools, in at least the international centers of the region, as early as MB IIB.

As for the southern Levant itself, here the world's first alphabet was invented sometime during the MB II, the individual signs of which were apparently derived from monosyllabic Egyptian hieroglyphs though the language recorded was West Semitic. Even though the earliest known alphabetic texts were found at Serabit el-Khadem in the western Sinai (by Flinders Petrie), we might assume that the alphabet was actually invented earlier in an urban center in the Levant, perhaps at Byblos or Gaza.[30] It is the introduction of the alphabet that provides one of the best witnesses to the emergence of a local Canaanite culture out of independent cultural streams from north Syria, the Phoenician coast and Egypt that penetrated the southern Levant throughout the Middle Bronze Age.

Middle Bronze Age culture began as a relatively short period

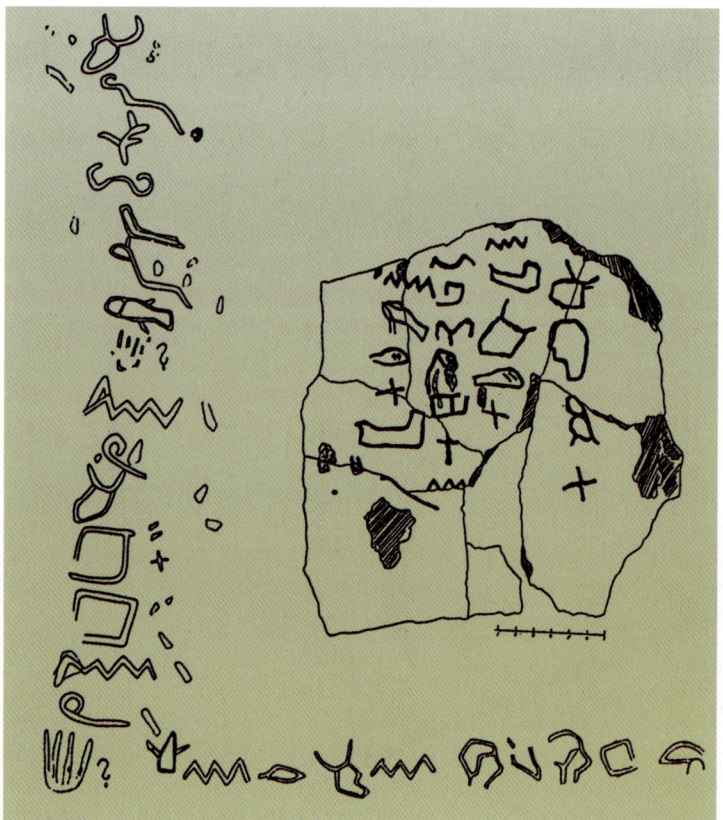

*Inscriptions in Proto-Canaanite alphabetic signs, from Serabit el-Khadem. (Ada Yardeni)*

*Remains of the Middle Bronze Age city of Shechem are easily visible from the summit of Mount Gerizim to its south. The curve of the strong MB wall can be seen on the left, connected to the main city gate. The middle of the excavated area is dominated by the thick walls of the temple tower, its door opening toward the east (right). This building likely served as the citadel of the city.*

of small, unwalled settlements which quickly became fortified city-states, most of which were surrounded, like those of EB, by smaller dependent villages. This settlement pattern is first seen on the coast north of the Yarqon River (e.g., Aphek and Acco) and in the northern connecting valleys (Jokneam, Megiddo, Shimron and Beth-shean) in MB IIA. Artifacts found at these sites are reminiscent of objects associated with Byblos and sites on the Orontes, providing evidence that the initiative for the rise to urbanization came from the north. The next phase of urbanization pushed inland to sites such as Laish (Dan), Hazor, Shechem, Shiloh and Gezer, while by MB IIB revived city-states could be found throughout the entire country, including the southern hills (Jerusalem, Hebron and Tell Beit Mirsim), the Negev (Tell el-'Ajjul and Tell el-Far'ah South) and Transjordan (e.g., Tell Hammam). By the seventeenth century B.C. many village sites in the southern Levant had disappeared, suggesting that the city-state complex gained strength at the expense of rural settlements. In seems as though by the end of MB IIB key regional cities such as Hazor, Shechem and Sharuhen (Tell el-Far'ah South) controlled extensive landed blocs, each of which was composed of smaller, individual urban areas.

All of the important urban centers in the Middle Bronze Age were fortified. City walls in MB II generally continued EB wall-building traditions, with the significant addition of earthen ramparts and/or a glacis to further strengthen urban defenses. Hazor, Laish,

*The MB II gates at Ashkelon (left) and Dan (right) are the oldest arched gates in Canaan. Their construction technique was different. The arch of the Ashkelon gate was made by gradually increasing the slope of the bricks of the attached city wall, while the arch of the gate at Dan was made by angling bricks individually. The gate at Ashkelon collapsed in antiquity; that at Dan survived, partly because of its superior construction technique and partly because it was intentionally buried after only a century of use.*

*The eastern gate of Middle Bronze II Shechem is unique. Access through the gate was apparently controlled by doors that slid into and out of the gaps formed by the paired megalithic stones in each of its corners.*

*(below) The ten standing stones at Gezer remain a sentinel over the coastal plain beyond. A single stone socket was uncovered next to the stones, perhaps as a place for water libations. The purpose of the stones is unclear: they likely memorialized some kind of a covenant, though whether it was made with deities, kings or city states is unknown.*

Shechem, Tel Batash (Timnah) and Ashkelon, for instance, were surrounded by ramparts. These were huge sloped mounds of earth which created a kind of crater (or partial crater) in which the city developed. The rampart at Shechem was faced with stones to give it additional strength. The largest and strongest fortified city in the southern Levant was Hazor, with a twenty-acre upper city and a 180-acre lower city founded in MB IIB protected by ramparts. A glacis was a half-rampart sloped on an average of 30 degrees, constructed of alternating layers of stone, brick and packed earth adjacent to the outside of the city wall. Cities with a glacis include Taanach, Megiddo, Shiloh, Jaffa, Gezer, Jericho and Lachish. The glacis not only supported the city wall but hindered the easy approach of an enemy and helped to prevent it from being undercut. Both ramparts and glacis forever changed the shape of ancient sites, giving them the classic "tell" shape seen today.

The gates of the walled MB II cities were typically symmetrical, straight axis structures flanked by projecting towers. The width of their entrances were on average 2.5 to 3.0 meters, more than sufficient for chariots which by MB IIB had become an important means of intercity transport. Two or three inward-jutting piers are typically found along each of the inward walls of MB II gates, creating one or two chambers on each side. Representative gates have been found at Laish (Dan), Acco, Hazor, Shechem, Megiddo, Beth-shemesh and Tell el-Far'ah South. Earlier examples of similar gates have been found in north Syria, providing additional evidence of an influx of northern populations into the area in MB II. Of special note are MB II mud brick arched gates which were built as part of the rampart system at both Laish (Dan) and Ashkelon. These, too, seem to be of north Syrian origin. The east gate at Shechem, however, is totally unique, with four sets of megalithic stones, one set at each of the gate's corners into which sliding doors may have been inserted.

Structures within the walls of MB II cities included dwellings, larger administrative or palatial buildings, and cult sites or temples. Dwellings show a natural development from semi-nomadic homesteads, with rooms located around an open, central courtyard similar to tents pitched facing one another. Larger, more complex buildings followed the same basic plan. The city palace was located at the central or highest part of the city, as is typical for all later periods. Some cities show evidence of city planning in the layout of the streets, which could run parallel to the curve of the wall (e.g., Megiddo) or straight, with right-angle intersections (Tell el-'Ajjul). Further planning can be seen in the remains of city drainage systems (at Hazor) and systems to channel and store fresh water. Jerusalem, a strongly fortified city in MB II, perhaps offers the best example of the latter. The city boasted a series of underground water channels that brought water from the city's Gihon Spring to storage reservoirs suitable for public access. While artifactual remains attesting to private religious activities have been found at various sites (e.g., metal figurines depicting the male storm god Hadad and the female fertility and astral deities), it is monumental structures that give weight to the strength of MB urban religious culture. These include the open air cult site at Gezer with ten large standing stones (maṣṣeboth), and the imposing temple towers at Hazor, Megiddo and Shechem. These temple towers are among the most impressive of all of the buildings of the entire second millennium B.C. Their overall shape is similar to buildings found in north Syria (Ebla, Alalakh and Ras Shamra) and at the Hyksos capital of Avaris (Tell ed-Daba'a) in the east Nile Delta. It consists of a long room fronted by a broad porch flanked by strong towers that lead to an inner sanctuary which was supported by pillars, all on a straight axis with wide entrance doors. The walls of the temple tower at Shechem were four meters thick.

The introduction of the fast potter's wheel in MB II allowed for new, thinner and more elegant vessel shapes. Characteristic MB shapes include globular jars and jugs, sharply carinated (angular) thin bowls, large flat bowls, deep kraters with handles attached to the rim, piriform juglets (i.e., small vessels with a slender body and high shoulders) and large, two-handled storage jars. MB IIA vessels were often decorated with a highly burnished red slip, which gradually gave way in MB IIB to a white or creamy slip. Of special note during late MB IIA and early MB IIB are Tell el-Yahudiyeh juglets, decorated with geometric incisions filled with rubbed lime. These vessels were made in the southern Levant and imported to Egypt (Tell el-Yahudiyeh in the southeastern Nile Delta), where they were first recognized in archaeological contexts by Flinders Petrie. Toward the very end of MB IIB Cypriot imports begin to be seen at Canaanite sites. As for objects of art, many were made locally in foreign styles, mimicking similar objects from Egypt, North Syria and Mesopotamia. These include bone-inlaid wooden boxes, faience and alabaster vessels, cylinder seals, figurines and jewelry.

The perfection of techniques of casting bronze (with 5–10% tin) led to significantly improved tools and weapons in MB. The duckbill axe used in MB IIA gave way to longer chisel-shaped axes by MB IIB. Daggers were ribbed for additional strength. Such weapons, together with the introduction of the war chariot, turned the fortified MB Canaanite city-states into mini-war machines, able to jostle each other for local supremacy or on behalf of a larger power. The region as far north as the Jezreel Valley came under the economic and political control of the West Semitic Hyksos who ruled from Avaris during MB IIB. Further north, Galilee was largely subject to Hazor which in turn was strongly influenced by cultural, economic and political realities of north Syria.

The Middle Bronze Age came to an end at the same time that the Hittites made incursions into north Syria from central Anatolia and the Hyksos fell to a native Egyptian dynasty (the 18th) in the Delta. The Egyptians under Ahmose chased the Hyksos back across the Sinai to their homeland, destabilizing the structure of the Canaanite city-states in the process. Most of the MB cities were destroyed at about the same time (c. 1600–1550 B.C.), though the MB cultural heritage and integrity of many of the MB city-states continued into the Late Bronze Age.

**Biblical Connections.** Ties between the Middle Bronze Age in the southern Levant and the Bible are inferential, at best contextual, and highly debated. Most scholars who accept the patriarchs as historical figures place them in the eighteenth and seventeenth centuries (MB IIB) on the basis of a biblical chronology that gives 430 years between Jacob and Moses (Ex 12:40) and a date of the Exodus that is contemporary with Rameses II.[31] Still, because the lifestyle of the patriarchs was of a type that is not archaeologically recoverable, we cannot expect that anything specifically related to Abraham, Isaac, Jacob or Joseph will ever be found. On the other hand, cities mentioned in the patriarchal narratives such as Shechem (Gen 12:6; 33:18; 37:12), Bethel (Gen 12:8; 13:3; 28:19; 35:1), Hebron (Gen 13:18; 23:2; 35:27; 37:14), Gerar (Gen 20:1; 26:1), Dan (Laish; Gen 14:14) and Salem (=Jerusalem; Gen 14:18) are known to have been sophisticated, strong city-states in MB II, hence setting an economic, social and political context for the patriarchs' interaction with them. One might assume, for instance, that Abraham's right to build altars near Shechem and Bethel (Gen 12:6–8) was in part won from the kings of those cities who saw in Abraham a potential ally. The interface between semi-nomads and urban centers that is seen in Genesis is reminiscent of a similar socio-economic symbiosis known from the Mari texts, as is the idea of semi-nomads moving from one city-state to another, sometimes settling down for a number of years. Archaeological evidence of all kinds also attests to a clear increase in cultural and economic ties between Egypt and the southern Levant, setting the backdrop for the patriarchs' natural move to the Delta in times of famine.[32] Other sociological and cultural ties between the patriarchal narratives and the MB II-era cultures of the ancient Near East have also been made, including those of marriage, adoption and inheritance customs, business agreements involving herding rights and forms of treaties attested in cuneiform texts from Mari (eighteenth century B.C.) and Nuzi (though further away and in the fifteenth century).[33] Taken together, evidence such as this is suggestive and contextual, though sufficient to set the stage for the beginning of the biblical story.

*Wall painting, 19th century B.C., from a tomb in Beni Hasan depicting a caravan of people from the Levant journeying to Egypt. This image represents the process by which populations from Canaan migrated to the Egyptian Delta throughout the Bronze ages.*

# The Late Bronze Age (c. 1550–1200 B.C.)

**Basic Characteristics.** The Late Bronze Age (LB) was an age of Egyptian dominance in Canaan. This was the period of Egypt's New Kingdom (18th–20th Dynasties), a time of Pharaoh Triumphant[34] in which Egypt anchored its imperialism in Canaan by a series of permanent, standing garrisons housed in Egyptian-style fortresses strategically located at key sites such as Gaza, Megiddo and Beth-shean. In terms of written records, the Late Bronze Age is the best documented period of Canaan until Roman times. Pharaohs like Thutmose III, Amenhotep III, Seti I, Rameses II, Merneptah and Rameses III left detailed accounts of their campaigns in the Levant, including lists of cities conquered and often destroyed. Another witness to this dynamic period are the 381 Amarna texts dating to the reigns of Amenhotep III and his son, Amenhotep IV

**MAIN LB SITES IN THE SOUTHERN LEVANT**

(Akhenaten), most of which were written in Canaan in a kind of hybrid Canaanite-Akkadian language using the cuneiform script. These texts offer a unique window into the Canaanite economy, society and politics during the the mid-fourteenth century B.C.[35] Twenty-seven Canaanite cities and twenty-five Canaanite rulers are mentioned in the Amarna texts by name, providing a rather personal view of the comings and goings of Egyptian control in the land during the period. From sources such as these one might emphasize the power that the pharaohs brandished to keep Canaan in the Egyptian orbit and come up with a picture of a weakened, subservient land. Or, one might stress the economic opportunities that grew from the control of a single political overlord and which

fostered linkages by which everyone benefited. The archaeological evidence can be read both ways.

There is enough historic and archaeological data to divide the Late Bronze Age into three periods: LB I (c. 1550–1400 B.C.) which saw the reestablishment of Egyptian control in Canaan following the overthrow of the Hyksos and destruction of Canaanite cities at the end of the Middle Bronze Age; LB IIA (c. 1400–1300 B.C.) which includes the Amarna Period; and LB IIB (c. 1300–1200 B.C.), the Ramesside Period which, in most estimations, was the time of the Exodus. That many of the important sites in Canaan have distinct material remains from all three LB periods implies that this was an unsettled time, with Egyptian campaigns, skirmishes between city-states (especially in the Amarna Period) and raids by and on semi-nomads all contributing to the complexity of the archaeological record.

Most of the urban sites destroyed at the beginning of the Late Bronze Age were not rebuilt until LB II. Those that were tend to reveal the same or similar architectural plans that they had in MB IIB, though at a less sophisticated or elaborate level. That the period saw a general decline of urbanization is clear; the extent that this was so at any given site remains a matter of debate. At the same time, artifactual remains suggest that LB II was also the high point of Canaanite culture. Perhaps a model that focuses on a renewal of Canaanite life in a few key cities at the expense of the rest of the land is helpful.

The basic Canaanite city-state structure of MB IIB was preserved in the region during the Late Bronze Age, especially on the coast and in the larger inland valleys, all under the umbrella of Egyptian vassalage. With advances in technology related to land and sea travel (the chariot, navigation and ship building), the routes and resources of the southern Levant became a ready source of revenue for the ravenous appetite of the Egyptian New Kingdom. The pharaohs favored the growth of places in Canaan that protected and fostered the economic interests of Egypt. These included a string of fortresses across the northern Sinai (the Horus Road or the Way to the Land of the Philistines; Ex 13:17) ending at Deir el-Balah and Gaza; a line of new ports from Gaza to Phoenicia (Tel Mor, Tel Michal, Tel Nami, Shiqmona and Tell Abu Hawam); and fortresses and/or administrative centers situated to control the international routes leading inland. The location of most of the larger sites in Canaan shows that the focus of urban settlement in the Late Bronze Age was along the coast (Gaza, Ashkelon, Ashdod, Jaffa, Aphek), in the Judean Shepehlah (Lachish, Gezer and Timnah) and in the major inland valleys (Dothan, Megiddo, Beth-shean, Pehel, Deir 'Alla and Hazor), and this irrespective of Egyptian interests. The two hundred acre mound of Hazor in particular should be noted as the largest and richest site in Canaan during the Late Bronze Age by far, well worthy of the label "head of all these kingdoms" (Josh 11:10).

Virtually all of the smaller MB II sites that had been located in the hill country were not rebuilt in LB, with Shechem, Tappuah, Bethel, and Tell el-Far'ah North the most important that survived. To date, LB remains at Gibeon, Hebron, Jericho, Ai (et-Tell) and Shiloh, all places mentioned in the accounts of early Israel's entrance into Canaan (Josh 2:1; 6:1; 7:2–5; 10:1–2; Judg 1:10), are sparse or nonexistent. The situation of Jerusalem is hotly debated, with the textual evidence from both the Bible (Josh 10:1; Judg 1:8) and the Amarna texts (EA 280, 285–288, 290) suggesting a strong, royal city while the archaeological evidence for such is largely lacking.[36] Still, scattered finds such as pieces of Egyptian figurines, alabaster vessels, capitals resembling the lotus capitals of Egypt's New Kingdom, and

*These two basalt lions from the Late Bronze Age city of Hazor seem to have been a matched set, positioned on either side of the entrance gate of a palace or temple. Their style is reminiscent of other carved lions found at sites in north Syria and speak of cultural contacts that linked Hazor to the north rather than to Egypt as was typical of Canaanite sites farther south.*

a small piece of a cuneiform tablet all suggest international interests in Jerusalem during the Late Bronze Age.[37] On the balance, the hill country was given over to more non-sedentary populations, with even the smaller, rural settlements that dotted the area through MB now almost completely lacking in the archaeological record.

Based on current archaeological data, most of the LB urban centers were largely or completely unfortified. These include centers of Egyptian interest such as Lachish, Megiddo and possibly Gezer. This made the Canaanite city-states submissive and unable to challenge Egyptian hegemony (by LB II the focus of Egypt's fight, and hence the need for strong fortifications, lay in Syria farther north). It also made them vulnerable to intercity strife. Cities that were fortified, were so with no discernible overall plan. The old MB fortification system of ramparts and glacis still existed to some extent, but with the notable exception of Hazor they no longer served to protect their cities (e.g., at Lachish houses and other structures were built on the rampart's outer slope). The MB IIB wall was restored at Shechem, but other cities were protected only by the outside walls of adjacent houses forming a kind of defensive perimeter. City gates were primarily restorations of the MB II gates (e.g., Hazor, Shechem and Megiddo), but at Megiddo there is no archaeological evidence that the gate was joined to defensive walls; this stands against Thutmose III's account of a siege.[38] The assessment of the Israelite spies in Canaan ("the cities are fortified and very large!" Num 13:28) should be seen as a comparison to the semi-nomadic tent encampments of the Sinai from which Joshua and company had come.

Methods of town planning in the Late Bronze Age are largely unknown due to insufficient evidence, but we might assume that the urban centers generally followed MB II plans. The best known examples of domestic architecture are the larger complexes built in the style of Egyptian domestic dwellings. These were square in shape with corner entrances and a central open courtyard, constructed with thick mud brick walls that could support a second floor. The remains of such buildings have been found along the Horus Road connecting Canaan to Egypt, at a number of sites on the southern coastal plain (Deir el-Balaḥ, Tell el-Farʿah South, Tell el-Ḥesi, Tel Seraʿ, Tell Jemmeh and Tel Mor), and inland at Beth-shean and Shechem. These "Egyptian residencies" were built to serve and protect Egyptian needs and likely functioned as administrative and economic centers, as well as garrison bases, for the region.

Egyptian-style temples have been found at Beth-shean and Lachish, as well as at Timnaʿ in the Negev where the Egyptians mined copper. These speak of Egyptian cultural and religious influences in the region. The Timnaʿ temple, dedicated to the goddess of mining Hathor, had a tent superstructure which was reminiscent in broad outline of the tabernacle. Other temples found at LB sites maintained local Canaanite or north Syrian architectural traditions. Of note are the monumental temple towers at Megiddo, Shechem and Hazor which continued the plans of their MB IIB predecessors. The temple tower from Hazor's Area H was particularly rich in finds, including twin lion orthostats carved in a north Syrian style that once guarded the building's entrance. Another temple from Hazor (Area C) included ten basalt stela, one of which depicted arms raised toward an image of the moon-god, as well as

**TEL HAZOR—THE MOUND AND EXCAVATION AREAS**

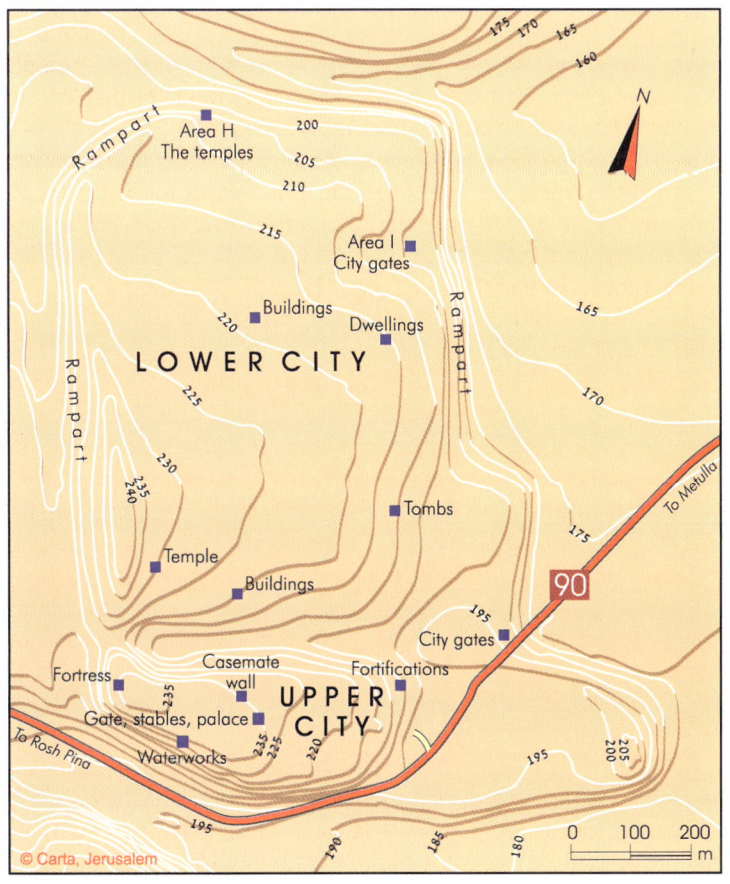

*The Merneptah Stela includes a poem commemorating Merneptah's victory over Canaan in the late 13th century B.C. The text specifically mentions the destruction of the cities of Ashkelon, Gezer and Yano'am, and the people group Israel being conquered by the pharaoh. (Cairo, Egyptian Museum)*

a statue of a seated male figure. The large, imposing building in the center of the upper city of Hazor, with a pillared entrance facing east and rooms of mud brick paneled in part with basalt, seems to have been either the primary temple or palace of the city.

Objects of worth found in LB Canaanite contexts include plaques and three-dimensional objects of ivory with Egyptian, Hittite and Assyrian forms; metalworking in copper, bronze, gold and silver, with tools, weapons, jewelry and figures of deities most prominent; and a great influx of fine imported pottery. All of this attests to open trade networks and consumers who were well off enough to afford the very best. These include white slip "milk bowls" from Cyprus, Mycenean bichrome vessels made on the fast wheel with precise and intricate designs, slender red-slipped bottles from Syria, and handleless vases and jars from Egypt. The Mycenean ware in particular seems to have been highly valued as collectable objects of art in LB II. Artifacts depicted on wall reliefs in Egypt include chariots of both Egyptian and Canaanite styles as well as the composite bow which, with a range of 400 meters, was one of the most effective weapons in the ancient world.

The Late Bronze Age in Canaan ended with the simultaneous waning of Egyptian control in the region and the arrival of the Sea Peoples from Anatolia and the Aegean. These included the Peleset (the biblical Philistines)[39] who settled on the southern coastal plain. The Sea Peoples were true invaders, bringing a new culture to the southern Levant that with the end of LB IIB appears in full force in the archaeological record. The disruption of the sea routes that connected the Levant with the Aegean is seen in the disappearance of Mycenean and Cypriot vessels at Canaanite sites in c. 1200 B.C. The fall of LB culture coincided with the general fall of civilizations across the ancient Near East and eastern Mediterranean at the end of the thirteenth century B.C. There is a corresponding rise in the number of small settlements found in the hill country of Canaan and Transjordan, particularly on the slopes facing the Jordan Valley out of the way of established city-states, at the very end of the Late Bronze Age. This may well reflect the emerging presence of the people group Israel, mentioned in the Merneptah Stela as having been conquered in Canaan in the fifth year of Merneptah's reign, at the very end of the thirteenth century B.C.[40]

**Biblical Connections.** The textual and archaeological record of the Late Bronze Age provides compelling evidence of the strength and sophistication of the Canaanite city-state structure which Israel encountered as they entered the land from the east. The Canaanites may well be portrayed as a base people by the writers of the Old Testament, but their material culture and ability to survive Egyptian domination gives evidence of a very sophisticated way of life that Israel could not, in the end, ignore.

The Amarna Age is of particular interest for biblical scholars, not only because it provides a living witness into international and local affairs in Canaan during the time leading up to Israel's appearance in the land, but because of the personality of Akhenaton and his advocacy of what is often described as a precursor to Mosaic monotheism.[41]

As to specifics related to Israel's appearance in Canaan, there is little archaeological evidence to be had. No Egyptian record of Israel's sojourn in Egypt survives, nor should we expect one in the overwhelmingly mud climate of the Delta. On the other hand, the mention of Rameses as one of the cities of the Delta that was built by Israel (Ex 1:11; cf. Gen 47:11) links the Exodus to LB IIB, the time of Egypt's nineteenth (Ramesside) dynasty. The nature of the wilderness wanderings as a reversion from settled life to tent-dwelling semi-nomadism ensures that nothing archaeologically recoverable from those years will ever be found. Though the list of cities conquered by Joshua does not fit the archaeological data of what was necessarily destroyed at the end of LB IIB, a careful reading of the biblical account indicates that hardly any of the cities conquered were actually destroyed and hence identifiable in the archaeological record anyway.[42] Of more concern is that to date, there is little to no archaeologically recoverable material from Jericho, Ai, Gibeon and Hebron, all cities that factor into the biblical account of Joshua's conquest of Canaan, thus indicating that they were not even inhabited during LB. A similar situation attains for Jerusalem, Gezer and even Byblos (Gubla / Gebal), each of which is portrayed as a prominent royal city in the Amarna Texts though the corresponding fourteenth-century strata are also largely lacking in the archaeological record. We should note that a fragment of a cuneiform letter and a seal of the Amarna pharaoh Amenhotep III have now been found in Jerusalem, both of which corroborate the picture of the city as a royal city in the Amarna period and a leader of the southern coalition against Joshua (Josh 10:1–5). At the same time, the overall lack of clear dating patterns for the destruction layers of urban LB II Canaan makes it very difficult to correlate specific strata with known historic events. Hazor of course is the most notable exception. Here the complete and permanent destruction of the Bronze Age city by fire in the mid-thirteenth century B.C., followed by rude and sporadic settlement in Iron I, fits nicely with the biblical account that "Israel did not burn any cities that stood on their mounds (i.e., tells) except Hazor alone, which Joshua burned" (Josh 11:13).

*El-Amarna letter 9. In this letter the king of Babylon assures Pharaoh Akhenaten that Canaan rightly is a vassal of Egypt. The archaeological record in LB Canaan supports this Egyptian tie.*

# Iron Age I (c. 1200–1000 B.C.)

**Basic Characteristics.** The advent of the Iron Age, so named because of the frequent appearance of iron objects in the archaeological record, is marked by the withdrawal of a permanent Egyptian presence from Canaan and the simultaneous disruption of established patterns of foreign trade with both Egypt and the Aegean. The transition between LB and Iron I is not consistent in the archaeological record but rather marked here and there by the disappearance of Cypriot and Mycenean IIIB pottery imports, even in some of the cities that were rebuilt along LB lines. In the vacuum left by Rameses III's defeat at the hands of the Philistines in the third decade of the twelfth century B.C., several smaller people groups were able to establish independent identities in Canaan; which many scholars view as having been emergent Israel.

Some of the cities in Canaan which were destroyed at the end of the Late Bronze Age were rebuilt along similar LB lines. These include Megiddo, Beth-shean, Tel Sera' (Ziklag), Tell el-Far'ah South, Shechem and Lachish, places in areas that historically had the most persistent Egyptian presence. While those in the south were fairly quickly incorporated into the orbit of Philistine or Israelite material culture, Megiddo and other cities in the Jezreel Valley and on northern (Acco) coast such as Tell Abu Hawam, Tell Keisan and Achzib were transformed by the eleventh century into the beginnings of a distinctive Cypriot-oriented Phoenician culture.

Most noteworthy in the archaeological record of Iron I is the arrival of the Peleset (Philistines) and other Sea Peoples such as the Tjekker and Sherden who settled along the south Levantine coast. The biblical and archaeological records both indicate that the Philistines originated in the Aegean, specifically Caphtor (Crete) and/or southern Greece (Amos 9:7; Jer 47:4). The battle reliefs found on the outside northern wall of Rameses III's funerary temple at Medinet Habu in Upper Egypt indicate that the Philistine warriors were accompanied by their wives and children, a clear indication of their intent to settle down. Of special note are the cities of the so-called Philistine pentapolis (1 Sam 6:4, 17): Gaza, Ashkelon, Ashdod, Gath (Tell es-Safi) and Ekron (Tel Miqne). The archaeological record shows Ashkelon, Ashdod and Ekron to have been strongly fortified in Iron I, and the Philistine sites in general were the largest urban centers in the area at this time. A Philistine presence has also been attested in the lowlands (the Judean Shephelah) from Gezer and Beth-shemesh in the north to Tel Eton in the south. The Yarqon basin (the area of modern Tel Aviv) was also dotted with Philistine sites. The most prominent of these were Aphek and Tell Qasile, the latter a planned urban center founded on virgin soil.

The appearance of a type of Mycenean IIIC1b pottery that was produced locally and not imported (with monochrome decorations on a light background) indicates a change in population in the southern Levant at the beginning of Iron I. Typical Philistine bichrome pottery appears a bit later, by the end of the second half of the twelfth century B.C. Philistine pottery is eclectic in design, with motifs derived from Mycenean pottery (e.g., birds, fish and geometrical shapes) that were painted in bichrome (red and black) colors on a light background, a style borrowed from the Canaanites. Sites with a high percentage of Philistine pottery in Iron I are concentrated on the southern (Philistine) coast between the Yarqon basin and Tell el-Far'ah South, in the northwestern Negev and in the Shephelah, though it never makes up more than 20% of the pottery assemblage found at any given site. A few examples of Philistine pottery have been found at sites throughout the hill country and in Transjordan, indicating Philistine commercial or

## MAIN IRON I SITES IN THE SOUTHERN LEVANT

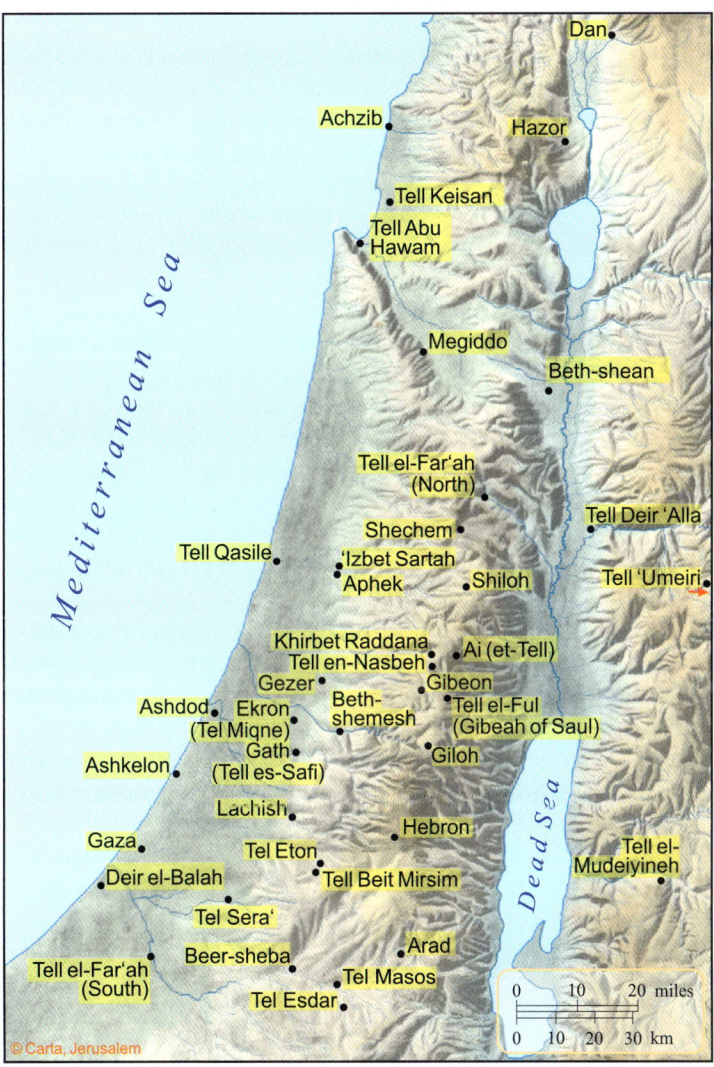

*Decorated Philistine jug from Tell es-Safi (Gath).*
(NEAEHL)

whether these helped to push Egypt out or simply benefited from its absence is a complex issue. In any case, peoples who were becoming known as Philistines, Phoenicians, Syrians, Ammonites, Moabites, Edomites and Israelites each began to develop somewhat distinctive material cultures during Iron I, suggesting a sense of local ethnicity. Some of these were invaders—the Philistines from afar, the Israelites from relatively near—who brought new material cultures with them. Others, like the Phoenicians, seem to have developed out of Bronze Age coastal Canaanite culture. It is possible to organize the archaeological data of Iron I into three base-line categories: a residual Canaanite culture at established urban sites on the northern coast and large inland valleys; an intrusive Philistine culture on the southern coast and in the adjacent lowlands; and a highlands culture *(left to right) Iron I cult stand with birds and serpents; anthropoid coffin lid (both from Beth-shean), and "Ashdoda" figurine from Ashdod (NEAEHL). Objects like these attest to the creativity that the Philistines brought to Canaan.*

military activity with other area populations.

The Philistines of Iron I exhibited a rich and creative material culture that speaks to their power and sophistication as heirs of the Egyptian presence in coastal Canaan. Unlike that of Bronze Age Canaan, Philistine material culture was not static, but exhibited a mixture of Aegean, Egyptian and local Canaanite cultural traits, making it a veritable laboratory of assimilation. Many luxury items of alabaster, ivory and metal have been found in Philistine archaeological contexts. These include clay offering stands topped by bird-shaped bowls (e.g., at Tell Qasile) and the "Ashdoda" figurine of a reclining lady in the form of a chaise lounge from Ashdod. The earliest iron objects from Canaan, a sword from Tell el-Far'ah South and a knife from Tell Qasile, were found at Philistine sites, providing tangible corroboration of the Bible's assertion that the Philistines had a reputation for metal working (1 Sam 13:19–22). Another set of noteworthy finds in Philistine contexts at Deir el-Balaḥ and Beth-shean are large, cylindrical anthropoid coffins of clay, the lid of each of which was embossed with a primitive view of the face of the deceased. The Philistine temple site at Tell Qasile is interesting in that it has the remains of three superimposed temples, each with a different architectural plan, over the course of just 150 years. This is in stark contrast to the Canaanite practice of preserving temple plans for centuries. The main room of the latest Qasile temple was supported by two columns, reminiscent of the house of Dagan in the last episode of the Samson story (Judg 16:23–30).

By noticeable contrast, hill country sites in Iron I Canaan exhibit a very different material culture, no doubt reflecting significant differences in social structure and ethnic identity among their inhabitants. Although the data is neither complete nor internally consistent, it is widely agreed that there was a sharp upward spike in the number of small (c. one acre), unwalled sites in central Canaan in Iron I, over 90% of which were on sites or in places not settled in the Bronze Age. These were concentrated first in the Jordan Valley and the eastern, drier approaches to the central hill country of Ephraim, Manasseh and Benjamin (the area between the Jezreel Valley and Jerusalem east of the watershed). Over the course of Iron I this settlement pattern spread over the watershed to the limestone hills facing west, to the southern hills and the Negev basin, and into the limestone hills of Galilee. The hills of Transjordan between the Yarmuk and Arnon canyons (Gilead, Ammon and Moab) also saw a similar pattern of new settlement in Iron I. Sites of note include Tell en-Naṣbeh (Mizpah), Tell el-Ful (Gibeah of Saul), Gibeon, Ai (et-Tell) and Shiloh on or near to the central watershed; Arad, Beer-sheba, Tel Masos and Tel Esdar in the Negev; but also Hazor, where the massive Canaanite city was replaced by poor, unwalled remains. Similarly at Shechem, where the LB city gave way to a sequence of two poorer settlements in Iron I. While most of the new sites appeared in areas somewhat distant from traditional Canaanite centers, others were nearby (e.g., 'Izbet Ṣarṭah just east of Aphek). Altogether hundreds of such sites have been surveyed, and many excavated. Most exhibit a single economic level that was rather rudimentary and poor. Taken together, they correspond to an overall rise of population in the hill country following the withdrawal of Egypt from Canaan.

As a whole, these sites reveal several distinctive features that have been often understood as Israelite:

- Settlements with layouts reminiscent of tent encampments in that the individual dwellings were arranged in a ring forming the perimeter of the site. The interior of the settlement area was left open, perhaps for flocks. Examples are found at 'Izbet Ṣarṭah, Giloh, Tel Masos and Beer-sheba.
- "Pillared houses," the beginning of what would become the classic Iron II "four-room house." These structures consisted of square or rectangular spaces divided by pillars into roofed and unroofed rooms typically extending perpendicularly from a broad room in the back, some with a second storey. Archaeologists debate their origins, some suggesting that this housing type was a change (devolution) from Egyptian courtyard-style residencies of LB and others holding that they were an evolution from semi-nomadic ("Bedouin") tents. Examples include dwellings found at Tel Masos, Giloh, 'Izbet Ṣarṭah, Shiloh, Khirbet Raddana, Ai. Monumental and public buildings are virtually unknown in Iron I hill country sites.
- An increase in the use of plastered cisterns, especially at sites in the drier hills (e.g., Ai/et-Tell, Khirbet Raddana).
- An abundance of round, stone-lined silos sunk into the ground at many sites, including Tell Beit Mirsim, Tell en-Naṣbeh (Mizpah), Shiloh, Dan, Hazor, Tell Deir 'Alla and Beer-sheba.
- The use of terraces on the hard limestone slopes of the central hill country, first appearing in Iron I.
- Collared-rim storage jars. These are large (1.2 meters high), ovoid pithoi with a ridge resembling a collar just below the rim, very common in the hills between the Jezreel Valley and Hebron. In similar Iron I sites in Galilee the pithoi have a broader, higher neck and no collar.
- A pottery repertoire that is rather poor, without a large variety of forms and largely undecorated, all in stark contrast to Philistine pottery.
- The virtual absence of pig bones in hill country sites, whereas pig bones are common in Philistine contexts and somewhat so in Canaanite contexts throughout the country in MB II.

Many scholars tend to call this configuration of hill country material culture "Israelite" on the strength of the biblical account of Israel entering Canaan from the east just prior to Iron I. However, it must be remembered that there were numerous groups settling in the southern Levant at the same time, both east and west of the Jordan Valley. Moreover, many of these features have also been found in non-hill country areas on both sides of the Jordan, and/or in other time periods. The question as to whether this change of material culture represents the arrival of newcomers as it clearly does for the Philistines, or is rather a reversion of Bronze Age urban culture to more semi-nomadic patterns, is hotly debated.

Iron I is, in essence, a precursor to Iron II rather than a preserver of the cultural forms of LB. While many of the smaller Iron I sites were abandoned or destroyed by the end of the eleventh century B.C., others survived to develop into fortified cities in Iron II (Tell el-Farʿah North/Tirzah, Tell en-Naṣbeh/Mizpah, Tell Beit Mirsim, Hazor, Beer-sheba and Arad). This concentration of hill country population into a relatively few number of sites corresponds to the rise of a centralized Israelite kingdom.

**Biblical Connections.** The Bible is clear in its assertion that the ancestors of ancient Israel were semi-nomadic pastoralists (Gen 13:3–7; 46:34; 47:3–4; Num 20:19; 32:1; Ps 78:52) and that they came from the east (Abraham, Jacob, Moses and Joshua). Their overall lifestyle and interactions prior to becoming sedentary were analogous to the Shasu pastoralists of New Kingdom (LB) Egyptian records. These were tent-dwellers on the fringe of Canaan who interacted with urban society in seasonal symbiotic (usually) and hostile (sometimes) ways, sometimes taking refuge within areas of urban settlement if climactic or economic conditions permitted or demanded.[43] An origin such as this is consistent with the material culture of the Iron I hill country, which reveals semi-nomadic populations gradually becoming sedentary.

The material culture that is often associated with Israel's arrival in Canaan is similar to that of central Transjordan. Four-room houses are known from excavations at Tell ʿUmeiri near Madaba and Tell el-Mudeiyineh farther south in Moab, and the pottery repertoire is nearly identical in key diagnostic categories. It has also been shown that ancient Hebrew has key linguistic affinities with Moabite and

**TELL QASILE—PLAN OF THE IRON I TEMPLE COMPLEX**

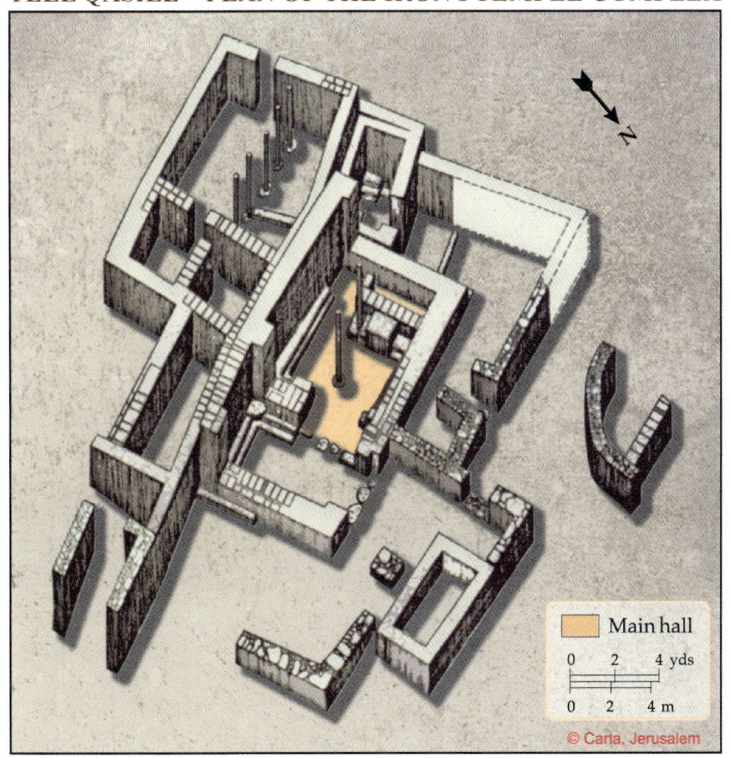

*At Shiloh, thin-walled buildings from Iron I were built adjacent to the outside of the imposing city wall from the Middle Bronze Age. Remains of a number of large collared-rim storage jars were found in these and other buildings nearby. A couple of modern reproductions of similar vessels grace the site today.*

Aramaic rather than coastal (Phoenician) Canaanite, suggesting its origins—and the origins of its speakers—in Transjordan.[44] Faust argues that visible ethnic distinctives within the archaeological record such as the lack of pig bones and the lack of decoration on pottery in the hill country served as a means of self-identification among the people groups that were becoming ancient Israel west of the Jordan Valley.[45] This is a reasonable assumption. The Philistines, by implication, set themselves apart from other emergent groups by developing their own set of markers.

With rare exception it is very difficult to correlate any specific Iron I remains with specific data (objects, structures or events) mentioned in the book of Joshua or Judges, even though the broad stroke settlement patterns are, on the whole, mutually consistent. The combined data suggests that it was Israel that first filled the hills on either side of the Jordan Valley, areas that were relatively empty and hence conducive to settlement. The location of the battles of Israel under Moses (Num 21:21–35; Deut 2:26–3:17) and Joshua (Josh 6:1–11:15) defined the outer perimeter of this area. The account of early Israelite settlement in Gilead and on the plateau around Medeba (Num 32:1–42) is consistent with the shared material culture in the hills on both sides of the Jordan Valley. As might be expected on archaeological grounds alone, the stronger Canaanite (and emerging Philistine) cities on the plains to the west and north would remain essentially outside of Israel's control for the next two centuries (Judg 1:27–36). Those that were destroyed and then rebuilt, marking the phase from LB to Iron I, attest to the persistence of the Canaanite urban ideal with which the biblical writers interacted throughout the Iron Age. The poor remains atop the destruction of the LB city of Hazor seem to fit the Bible's battle sequence; first an account of the conflagration of Hazor by Joshua (Josh 11:11, 13), then a battle in the Jezreel Valley against displaced Hazor forces (Judg 4:1–16). A destruction layer dated to the early eleventh century at Shechem echoes the account of Abimelech's failed kingship (Judg 9:1–57), while the temple tower of El-berith that features in the account (Judg 9:46–49) may well have been the old MB II and LB structure. Finally, the rise of the number of small hill country settlements that appears first in Ephraim and Manasseh reflects the emphasis on the prominence of settlement activity specifically in those hills as related in the books of Joshua and Judges (Josh 8:30–35; 17:14–18; 18:1; 24:1–33; Judg 7:2–8:1; 9:1–57; 12:1–6).

# Iron Age II (c. 1000–586 B.C.)

**Basic Characteristics.** Iron II is the time of the Israelite monarchy, the period when most of the events described in the Old Testament took place. More archaeological data exists for Iron II than for any preceding period due to the larger number of sites excavated as well as the larger total area of Iron II strata uncovered. Most importantly, scholars have access to numerous contemporary written documents (i.e., primary sources) that mention material cultures that can be found archaeologically. Chief among these for the land of ancient Israel is, of course, the Hebrew Bible. To be added to this are numerous royal inscriptions and other texts from Assyria, Babylon and Egypt, as well as documents produced locally and found in excavations of Iron II strata. Some of these are monumental inscriptions that record royal activities (e.g., the Mesha and Tel Dan stelae); others are more mundane such as letters, receipts, invoices or notations. Here the most important groups of ostraca (texts written on potsherds in ink) were found at Samaria (8th cent.), Lachish (late 8th cent.) and Arad (early 6th cent.). Other texts of importance for biblical scholars have also been found at Khirbet Qeiyafa (10th cent.), Tel Zayit (10th cent.), Meẓad Ḥashavyahu (7th cent.) and numerous other sites in Israel, Judah, Philistia, Edom, Ammon and Moab.[46] To these must be added hundreds of inscribed seal stones, seal impressions on jar handles, and bullae, clay seal impressions used to seal documents which themselves have not been preserved. These and other inscriptions provide invaluable information for the historian on the mechanisms of administration, economy, law, education and religion in Iron II. They also attest to the level of literacy among the peoples of Israel and their neighbors.

The interface of inscriptions and archaeological data in Iron II provides the first firm synchronisms for historic events in the land of ancient Israel. Most important is the destruction of Lachish by Sennacherib in 701 B.C., an event described three times in the Bible (2 Kgs 18–19; 2 Chron 32; Isa 36–37) as well as in numerous Assyrian sources both written and pictorial. This event has been fixed by a clear pottery context to Lachish level III. A similar synchronism dates the destruction of Jerusalem by Nebuchadnezzar of Babylon to 586 B.C. In contrast, though many other campaigns against Israel and Judah are mentioned in the Bible and in Assyrian, Babylonian and Egyptian texts (e.g., by Shishak and Shalmaneser III), it is difficult to correlate them with specific strata at any given site because the archaeological destruction record in Iron II is so active. Similarly the great earthquake at the time of Uzziah (Amos 1:1; Zech 14:5) might be correlated with the eighth century destructions of Hazor (level VI) and Lachish (level IV), though not with absolute certainty. A seal impression of Pharaoh Siamun found in a tenth century context at Gezer may indicate that this is the pharaoh who destroyed the city and then gave it as a dowry for his daughter's marriage to Solomon. However, because there are two tenth century B.C. destruction layers at Gezer the synchronism is not exact. Still, in spite of these "almosts," there is enough data in texts and the archaeological record to justify the term historical archaeology, or, in this case, biblical archaeology, for Iron II in particular.

Iron II can be divided into three sub-periods: Iron IIA (the tenth and ninth centuries B.C.); Iron IIB (the eighth century to 701 B.C.); and Iron IIC (701 B.C.–586 B.C.). These archaeological periods can be given exact dates because of firm synchronisms. In terms of changes in material culture, these divisions are a bit artificial in that developments in pottery typology can sometimes be distinguished by the quarter century.

Iron II was the second urban period for the southern Levant (the first was the Middle Bronze Age; the third will be the Roman and Byzantine periods), with thriving nation states that to some degree

*The Iron IIA gate at Gezer is the best preserved of the six-chambered gates in ancient Israel. Others have been uncovered at Megiddo and Hazor, all sites fortified by Solomon.*

developed regional variations in material culture. Large enough areas have been excavated at individual tells to allow archaeologists to reconstruct city plans (e.g., Beer-sheba, Tell en-Naṣbeh, Tell Beit Mirsim, Beth-shemesh, Megiddo and Samaria). The material culture of Iron II Israel was not particularly extravagant or creative, but it was functional. On the other hand, there are indications of clear international connections between Israel and other peoples of the ancient Near East in the archaeological record, including those of Egypt, Mesopotamia and Asia Minor. Because there is a larger amount of recovered material culture dating to the ninth century B.C. than there is for the tenth, and even more so for the eighth, the availability of data tends to skew the interpretive results in favor of the later periods.

There is an overall continuity of material culture from the tenth to the ninth centuries B.C. (the time of the United Monarchy to Ahab, to use the biblical chronology). This is seen in both building techniques as well as pottery assemblages. In recent years some scholars have tried to establish a Low Chronology by down-dating finds traditionally assigned to the tenth century B.C. into the ninth. One of the results is to have created a kind of vacuum of significant material cultural finds for the tenth century, taking hostage, in essence, the monumental building projects of David and Solomon described in the biblical record.[47] This in turn has prompted archaeologists to reexamine the material culture of all Iron IIA strata. The issue is not the change from Iron I to Iron IIA forms which indicate a corresponding change in settlement patterns from semi-nomadic and village structures to monarchy, but how early it happened.

Many of the small Iron I settlements in the southern Levant disappeared in Iron IIA, with the overall settlement pattern tending to coalesce back to established urban centers in the highlands and the Shephelah. This dip in the number of exposed, rural settlements was perhaps a natural response to a rise in regional or inter-tribal fighting, stimulating the need for populations to concentrate in regional centers. This in turn perhaps played a key role in state-formation.[48] Indeed, the most distinctive mark of Iron IIA is it's royal building projects. For a people rooted in semi-nomadic social and material culture, the shift was quite remarkable.

The most visible aspect of Iron IIA urbanization is city fortifications. Notable are six-chambered gates with front towers found at Hazor, Megiddo and Gezer. While the dimensions and construction techniques of these three gates varied, their overall idea is consistent with set of shared opportunities and needs, if not a unified plan. Casemate city walls dating to the tenth century have been found at Gezer, Hazor, Jokneam, 'En Gev, Tell en-Naṣbeh (Mizpah), Beth-shemesh, Khirbet Qeiyafa and Tell Beit Mirsim, and to the ninth century at Tell Bornat, Beer-sheba and the large towered enclosure at Jezreel. The fortifications at Gezer, Beth-shemesh, Khirbet Qeiyafa and Tell Beit Mirsim seem to indicate a defensive line in the Shephelah between the emerging states of Israel and Philistia. Massive solid city walls dating to the tenth century have been found at Ashdod, Beer-sheba, 'En Gev (at these last two the solid wall predates the casemate wall), Dan, Tel Malḥata, Megiddo and Tell en-Naṣbeh (here built over the casemate wall in the late tenth century), and solid walls were constructed at Hazor and Lachish in the ninth century. Though contested, it seems as though a solid wall connected to a four-chambered gate dating to the tenth century has also been found at the northern end of the oldest part of the walled city of Jerusalem.[49] The basic urban infrastructure of LB Jerusalem, including parts of the water system and city wall with its revetment (stepped stone structure) at the northern part of the city, was likely still functional in Iron IIA.[50] Tel Reḥov is a special case. Though archaeological evidence shows the Iron IIA

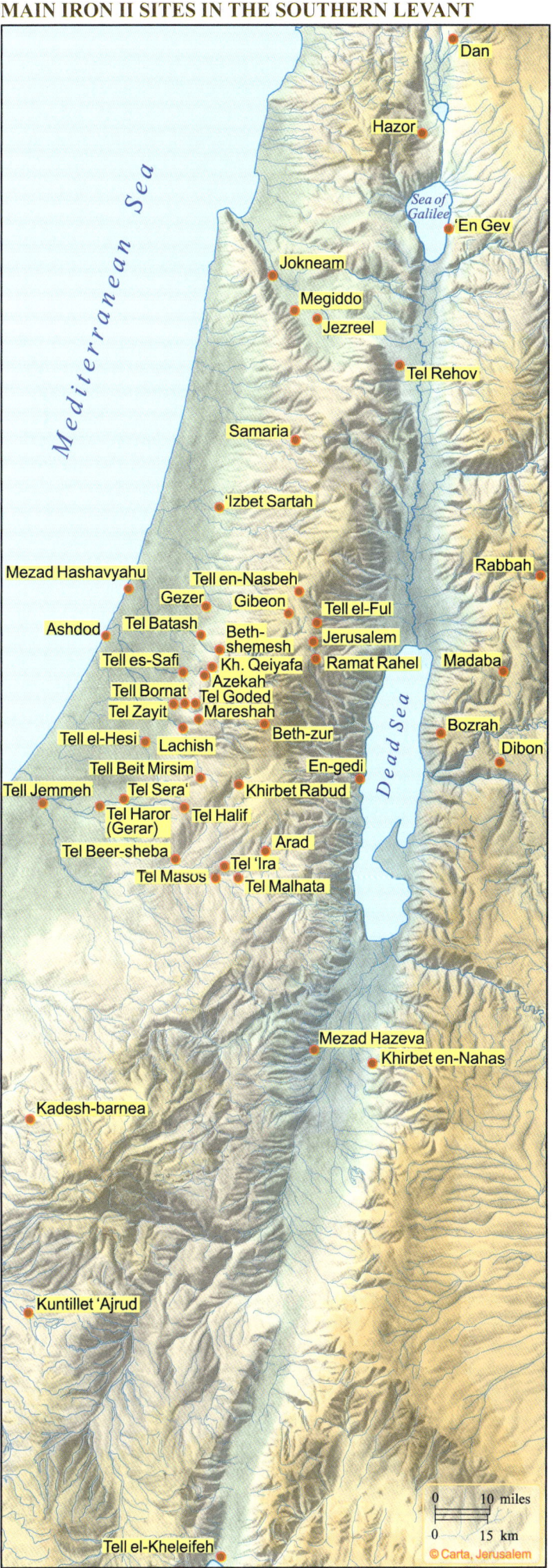

MAIN IRON II SITES IN THE SOUTHERN LEVANT

*Three tri-partite buildings have been found just inside the city gate of Iron IIB Beer-sheba. Similar buildings have been found at other major sites in ancient Israel and Judah. Though buildings like these at Megiddo have been interpreted as stables, it is more likely that all were storerooms or warehouses. If so, they indicate a kind of centralized control over distribution and supply lines at key sites in the land.*

*Set side-by-side like row houses, these four-room houses line the city street of Iron IIB Beer-sheba. Each included a broad room in the back that doubled as part of the city's casemate wall. Long rooms extended toward the street, divided by rows of columns. The "space syntax" of the four-room house seems to have been particularly appropriate for the economic and social interactions of Israelite village life.*

## TEL BEER-SHEBA—PLAN OF THE IRON II CITY

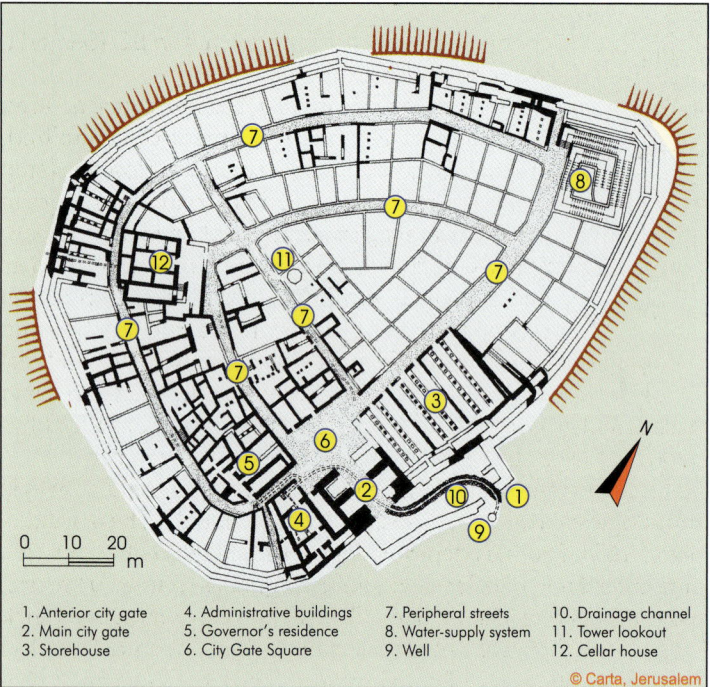

1. Anterior city gate
2. Main city gate
3. Storehouse
4. Administrative buildings
5. Governor's residence
6. City Gate Square
7. Peripheral streets
8. Water-supply system
9. Well
10. Drainage channel
11. Tower lookout
12. Cellar house

of adjacent four-room houses backed. One building contained a large, well-formed horned altar. Everything led to an open square at the city's inner gate, off of which the governor's house (a larger version of the four-room plan) and the city's pillared storerooms were located. A drainage canal led from nearby rooms out the city's double gate. The city water supply came from an enclosed, stepped installation within the walls, as well as an open well just outside the outer gate. Beer-sheba sat at the confluence of two major wadis which carried routes connecting it with the Negev, the coast, the Shephelah and sites in the southern hill country. It was, by all appearances, an administrative, economic, military, political and religious center in the Iron Age. Evidence of similar plans has been found at Lachish, Mizpah, Beth-shemesh and Tell Beit Mirsim, enough to suggest that the ring-road pattern was typical to regional urban centers in Iron II Judah.

There was an overall tendency to strengthen fortifications in the southern Levant toward the end of the eighth century, nicely corresponding to the increased Assyrian threat that with Sennacherib's campaign of 701 B.C. would bring about the transition from Iron IIB to Iron IIC. Most sites show evidence of city wall reinforcement in Iron IIB, with some casemate walls made solid (Hazor) and very thick walls being constructed around Tel Batash (Timnah) and the western hill of Jerusalem. Some sites show the addition of a steep glacis (Lachish, Beer-sheba, Tel 'Ira and Tel Ḥalif). City gates, however, tended to shrink in size, going from six chambers to four to two during the course of Iron II. Fortified sites appeared throughout the Shephelah in Iron IIB, as well as in the Negev basins, indicating well-planned western and southern Judean fronts. Their overall material culture reflects that of the southern hill country of Judah. The appearance of a few fortified sites in the harsh living conditions just west of the Dead Sea indicate centralized priorities on an eastern line as well. The dense pattern of Iron IIA forts in the Negev highlands does not seem to be reestablished in the eighth century, giving way to only a very few larger, stand-alone fortified sites at key spots on the network of international routes (Kadesh-barnea and Kuntillet 'Ajrud in the northeast Sinai, Meẓad Ḥaẓeva in the Rift south of the Dead Sea, and Tell el-Kheleifeh on the northern tip of the Gulf of Eilat). A series of forts or fortified towers maintaining line-of-sight connection throughout the hills surrounding and west of Jerusalem, as well as in the environs of Samaria, also speak of a centralized attempt at communication and control.

Many of the larger urban centers had sophisticated systems to transport and store water in Iron Age II. These typically made use of steps, tunnels, shafts and pools. Some linked the system directly to the aquifer (Hazor, Gezer and Gibeon). Others redirected the waters of the city's spring (Jerusalem and Megiddo). While many of these systems had their start in Iron IIA or before (the technology is difficult to date), they certainly played a defensive role in the face of the Assyrian threat.

The four-room house, which first appears in Iron I, became the standard, typical hill country dwelling by Iron IIB. Such structures are found in all types of sites from Jerusalem to small villages, for both private homes and public buildings. The widespread adoption of a floor plan which allows equal access to all living spaces of the house via a common, central space directly accessible from the street perhaps reflects a society with egalitarian ideals.

Iron IIB saw a flowering in literary creativity, especially as it related to national, spiritual and economic life. While some inscriptions are known from Iron IIA, there is a noticeable increase in writing through Iron IIB and C. Of note are the ostraca bearing notations of shipments of oil and wine to Samaria, the Siloam Inscription detailing the work of the men who hewed out the water tunnel beneath Jerusalem, and numerous vessels and bullae bearing ownership inscriptions. Chief among these are the Royal (LMLK, "to the king") seal impressions found on the handles of large storage jars for liquids at sites throughout Judah. The seals mention four cities: Hebron, Socoh, Ziph and *mmšt*. All date to the late eighth century B.C. (Lachish level III), and apparently have to do with a centralization of administration and economy related to Judah's war effort against Sennacherib.

Iron IIB also saw the start of a development of independent, regional material cultures throughout the region, seen most readily in pottery assemblages. These attest to ethnic and/or political divisions in the land. For instance, bowls found on the Phoenician coast and in western Galilee were made with extremely thin walls covered with a highly burnished, thick slip of alternating bands of colored red and yellowish-white. Imported to Samaria, this type of vessel carries the misnomer "Samaria Ware." Vessels made in the Samaria hill country and eastern Galilee are characterized by a burnished red slip, while those of the Judean hills, Shephelah

## TEL MEGIDDO—PLAN OF THE MOUND

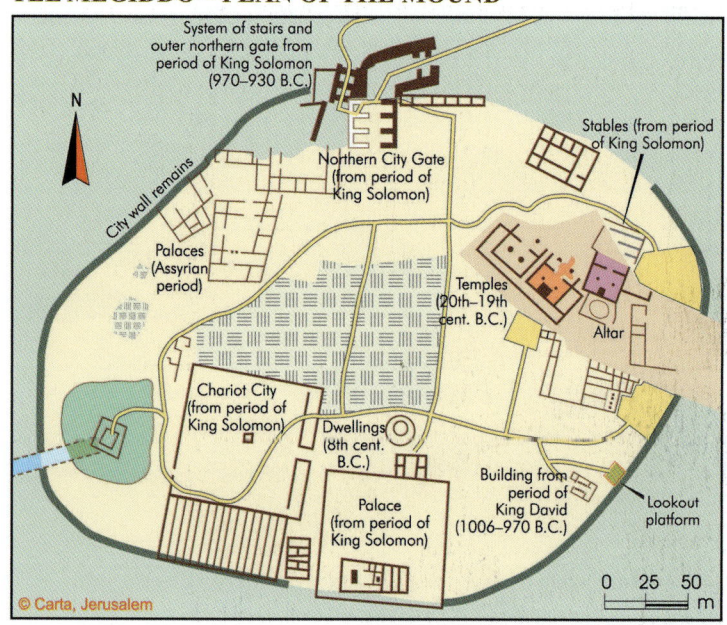

*Text of the Siloam Inscription. (Ada Yardeni)*

and the Negev are typically covered by a burnished orange-red slip. Pottery associated with the southern, Philistine coast is a bit degenerative from the classic Iron I forms, though certainly more creative than its counterparts in the hills.

To these should be added a growing presence of Assyrian material culture towards the end of Iron IIB. Here the most enduring forms are building and city plans. After the Assyrians conquered Megiddo and made it a regional capital, they rebuilt the city on a grid plan with palaces of the courtyard type (rooms around a central court). Similar palaces have been found in contemporary strata at Hazor, Tell Jemmeh and Tel Seraʻ (Ziklag) in the northern Negev, and Bozrah in Edom, all of which were located in regions of known Assyrian campaigns.

The widespread invasion of Sennacherib that marks the end of Iron IIB in 701 B.C. is seen in destruction layers at Lachish, Tel Batash (Timnah), Tell Beit Mirsim, Tel Haror (Gerar), Mareshah, Azekah, Tel Goded, Tell es-Safi (Gath), Tel Zayit and Ramat Raḥel. One might argue that Iron IIB ended in the Samaria hills a couple of decades earlier, when the Assyrians had conquered Galilee (in 732 B.C.) and then Samaria (721 B.C.). By his own account Sennacherib "laid siege to 46 strong cities, walled forts and countless small villages in their vicinity, conquering them by means of well-stamped (earth-) ramps and battering-rams brought near to the walls."[53] The remains of Lachish level III reveal evidence of the siege and destruction of the city that matches exactly Sennacherib's claims.

Iron IIC is characterized by the rebuilding of sites in Judah after the devastation of the Assyrian attack. Some cities were refortified with solid walls (Lachish, Tel Batash, Tel ʻIra; Beth-zur; Khirbet Rabud), while others had casemate walls (Arad, Kadesh-barnea, Tell el-Ful). Some Judean cities remained unfortified (Tell Beit Mirsim, En-gedi). Cities in Israel that remained under Assyrian control were also not fortified in Iron IIC (Samaria, Megiddo and Hazor).

Similarities in pottery assemblages at area sites attest to the reestablishment of centralized, monarchial control from Jerusalem. Rosette stamp seal impressions on jar handles found only south of Gibeon also suggest a centralization in the southern regions similar to that of the Royal (LMLK) seal impressions of Iron IIB. Of note is that sites on the coastal plain (e.g., Gezer), in the Samaria hills and throughout the northern valleys exhibited an Assyrian material culture until the late seventh century B.C., after which forms similar to those of Judah took over. This indicates a revival of Judean fortunes following the collapse of Assyrian hegemony in the region.

A clear increase in material culture of a religious nature, mostly from domestic contexts, is seen in Iron IIC Judah. These include pillar fertility figurines depicting females (Asherah) with unusually large breasts and detailed faces, animal figurines (primarily horses), and horned stone incense altars. The highest concentration of such finds was in Jerusalem. Many appear to have been deliberately broken, smashed or disfigured prior to the Babylonian campaign which brought about the end of Iron IIC in 586 B.C. Similarly, the Arad temple, which underwent several restorations throughout Iron II, went out of use in the last decades of the seventh century, two or three decades before the site was destroyed.

The end of Iron IIC can be seen in part with the violent destruction of many of the fortified cities of Judah in the early sixth century B.C., but also in the gradual influx of Edomite pottery into the Negev and southern hill country at about the same time.

**Biblical Connections.** It is with the synchronisms of Iron II that biblical archaeologists can finally move from context to specifics. The richness of the archaeological framework of Iron II provides ample opportunity to give texture and color to the biblical account of the period of the Israelite and Judean monarchies. There is far and away more material available for the period than can be mentioned here, and so a few illustrative examples must suffice.

The rise of urbanization in the Iron IIA highlands and Judean Shephelah at the expense of the rural settlements of Iron I, if explained as due to security needs rising from pressures on tribal groups, fits the rise of a newly established Israelite monarchy out of the less secure conditions of the time of the Judges. Much of the focus is on the transitional tenth century, and in that, on Jerusalem. Some scholars have tended to approach the nature of Israel's United Kingdom as "either-or": either the evidence supports the biblical account of Jerusalem as the urban capital of a unified, national kingdom, or it indicates something much less, a small tribal chiefdom in which Jerusalem was a "cow town" or an isolated fort. A more realistic approach might be to seek a middle ground under the working assumption that no centralized authority of any state or institution arrives full form, but rather builds to maturity with its material culture becoming "heavier" and hence more archaeologically visible in the process. Jerusalem of the tenth century B.C. is best viewed as the capital of a kingdom in the making, with some pieces in place and others on the way. The large, rough-hewn stone palace likely dating to the tenth century B.C. located at the northern end of the City of David, the oldest part of the walled city of Jerusalem, fits this model well. This structure, according to its excavator Eilat Mazar, was the palace of David. Remains of the palatial buildings constructed by Solomon haven't been found, although the biblical description of the buildings (1 Kgs

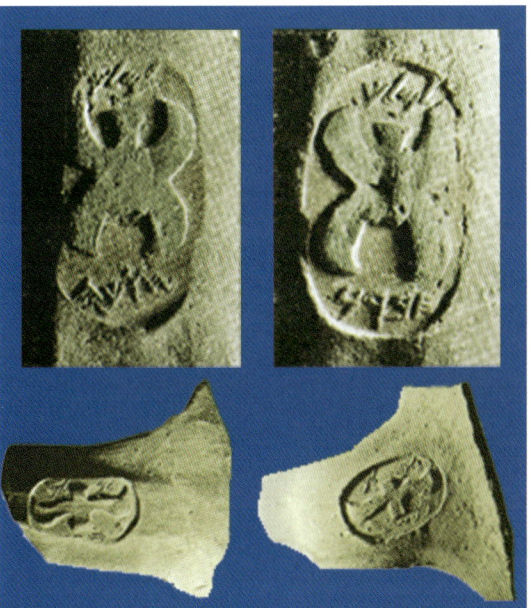

*Royal LMLK seals of (clockwise, from top left) Socoh, Hebron, Ziph and mmšt. (NEAEHL)*

## 'AIN DARA—PLAN OF THE TEMPLE

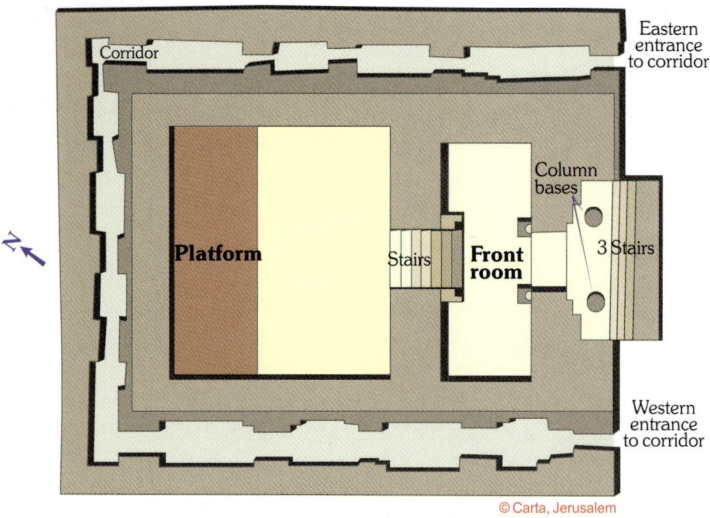

7:1–12) fits the north Syrian *bīt-ḥilāni* style uncovered at Megiddo. So too Solomon's temple: details of its "blueprint" provided in 1 Kings 6 indicate that it was designed and built according to known architectural plans from north Syria in general, and to a temple found at 'Ain Dara near Aleppo in particular.[54] Fine ashlar masonry typical to that found in later Israelite and Judean palaces is described in the biblical account of Solomon's building activities (1 Kgs 5:17–18), and the discovery of proto-ionic capitals brings to mind the description of engravings of palm trees in the Temple (1 Kgs 6:29, 32, 35).

The biblical narrative of the United Monarchy includes other impressive national building projects. Chief among these are the cities of Hazor, Megiddo and Gezer (1 Kgs 9:15–17). Even though details of the tenth century B.C. gates and walls uncovered at these cities vary in dimension and construction technique, the overall idea (six-chambered gates with projecting towers) is consistent enough to relate them to a unified effort under Solomon. Especially interesting are the Iron IIA strata at Gezer linked to Siamun, likely the pharaoh of 1 Kings 9:16 whose daughter Solomon married in connection with rebuilding the city. Tenth century fortified remains at Meẓad Ḥaẓeva can be identified with Tamar, a Solomonic outpost in the Rift Valley south of the Dead Sea securing the route between Jerusalem and the Red Sea (1 Kgs 9:17, 26–28). Just to the east at Khirbet en-Nahas near Feinan is evidence of copper mining activity dating to the tenth century, the most likely source of the copper Solomon's workmen used to make the bronze items for the Jerusalem temple (1 Kgs 7:13–47). Of additional note are the tenth century fortifications at Khirbet Qeiyafa in the Elah Valley, the earliest site in the Shephelah that was fortified in the Iron Age. This site in particular seems to have been related to the Israelite-Philistine conflict recorded in the David-Goliath story (1 Sam 17:1, 20), either as a Philistine outpost or the "circle of the camp" of Saul.[55] All told, the fortifications throughout Israel dating to the tenth century seem to indicate a set of conflicts on the borders of an expanding Israelite kingdom as expressed in the biblical narratives of David and Solomon.

Other Iron IIA fortifications mentioned in the Bible in connection with the early years of the Divided Monarchy have also been found in archaeological excavation. Particularly impressive is the solid wall of Mizpah (Tell en-Naṣbeh) erected by Asa to secure Judah's northern border against Israel (1 Kgs 15:22). Asa's efforts at Mizpah included a stronger city gate, large four-room houses appropriate for official administrative functions, and a number of grain silos, all of which attest to the site's economic and administrative role as a border town. Up in Israel, the moves of Omri and his son Ahab toward solidifying and expanding the kingdom are most visible in the fortifications of Samaria and Jezreel. Although the archaeological remains of Ahab's capital at Samaria are not well preserved, the strength and elegance of the site is beyond doubt. Ahab's magnificent palace of header-stretcher ashlar masonry set the architectural standard for similar royal palaces constructed subsequently in Judah (Ramat Rachel) and Ammon (on the citadel of Rabbah). The carvings of ivory which were found in excavation in Samaria as well as in Nimrud where they had been carried as booty by the Assyrians must have decorated Ahab's "ivory house", a structure that is mentioned with glorious contempt by the writers of 1 Kings 22:39 and Amos 3:15; 6:4. The fortress at Jezreel served not only as the second capital of Ahab's dynasty (1 Kgs 18:45–46; 21:1; 2 Kgs 8:29; 9:15; 10:1), but headquarters for the part of his chariot force which was engaged in continual battles with Aram-Damascus. The Mesha Stela (Moabite Stone), found on the site of Dibon in Moab, provides an alternate historical narrative of events in Transjordan following the death of Ahab (2 Kgs 1:1; 3:3–4). It and the Tel Dan Stela are the only texts from Iron II that mention the Davidic dynasty by name.

The increase in archaeologically visible material culture from the tenth to the ninth century, then even more so for the eighth, is to be expected as the states of Israel and Judah gained strength and importance in the southern Levant. The reestablishment of viable, though unfortified, rural settlements in addition to the larger established regional centers in Iron IIB indicates a maturation of the development of the kingdoms consistent with the biblical record of the growth of Israel and Judah. The complete demise of

*The Mesha Stela from Dibon, a Moabite text of the mid-ninth century B.C. that describes the conquest of Transjordan's Medeba Plateau by Mesha, king of Moab, following the death of Ahab.* (NEAEHL)

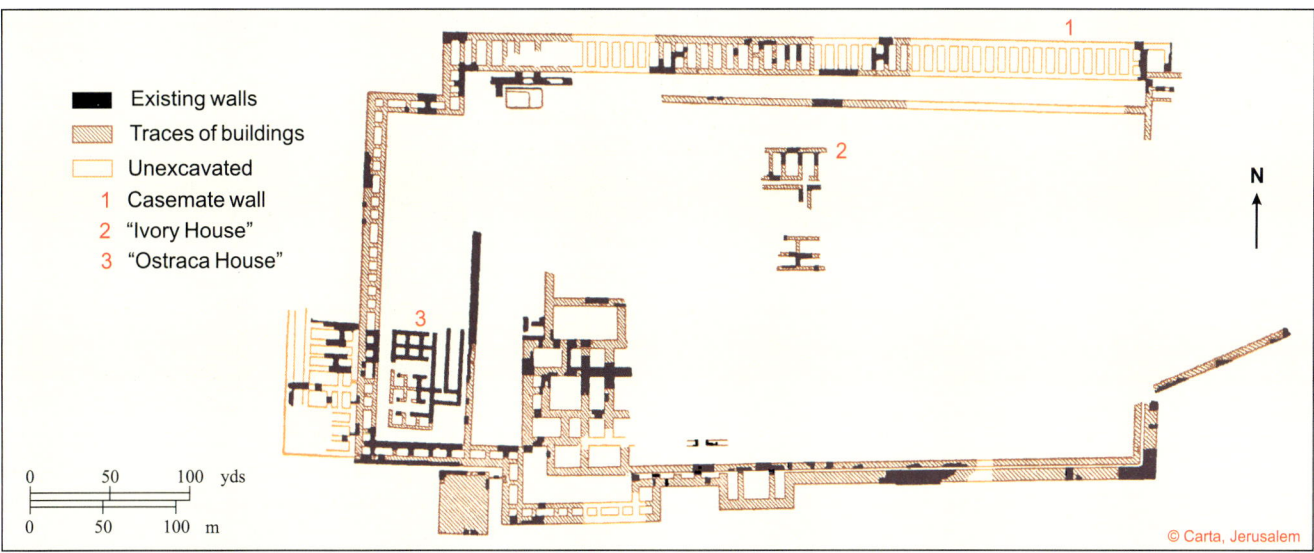

PLAN OF AHAB'S PALACE IN SAMARIA

- ■ Existing walls
- ▨ Traces of buildings
- ☐ Unexcavated
- 1 Casemate wall
- 2 "Ivory House"
- 3 "Ostraca House"

settlement in the southern Negev highlands is odd, but it too is at least consistent with the location of the "official" southern border of Judah at Beer-sheba (2 Kgs 23:8). The clear indication in the archaeological record that Iron IIB Beer-sheba was an organized, planned city suited for regional economic and administrative control fits its role as a border town, as Mizpah did farther north. A series of forts along the western shore of the Dead Sea and in Buqei'ah, a small plain just above, can be associated with Uzziah's efforts to strengthen the infrastructure of Judah (he "built towers in the wilderness," 2 Chron 26:10).

Archaeology has also shed important light on the issue of literacy in ancient Israel. While the number of written documents produced locally is far less than is known from the centers of empire in ancient Egypt, Mesopotamia and even north Syria, a growing body of texts found at sites in the southern Levant gives evidence that at least some levels of Israelite and Judean society were literate. Written documents produced or found at urban or state-sanctioned sites in Israel and Judah dating to Iron IIB and IIC are to be expected (e.g., the Samaria ostraca, Arad inscriptions, Lachish letters and bullae generally). They attest not only to sophisticated practices of state administration and record keeping but the presence of local scribal schools. More interesting, perhaps, are the texts written in Hebrew in the tenth century B.C. which have been found (and apparently were written!) at places far from the established Israelite centers of Iron IIA (e.g., Khirbet Qeiyafa, Tel Zayit, 'Izbet Ṣarṭah). The level of literacy in ancient Israel has a direct bearing on the processes by which many of the texts of the Bible were written, and provides a credible time frame for at least the start of the process.

The Assyrian invasions of the late eighth century B.C. are everywhere visible in the archaeological record. The Bible makes special mention of the Assyrian attack on Samaria (2 Kgs 17:5) and Lachish (2 Kgs 18:13, 17), together with all of the fortified cities of Judah (cf. Mic 1:8–16; Sennacherib mentioned that these numbered forty-six). Hezekiah's efforts to prepare Jerusalem for the Assyrian attack included strengthening the wall of the City of David (Isa 22:9), hewing "a pool and a conduit [by which he] brought water into the city" (2 Kgs 20:20) and erecting a 22-foot thick wall around the western hill of Jerusalem. To do so, he had to destroy houses that lay in the most defensible line (Isa 22:10). This, as well as the wall and tunnel in the City of David, have all been found in archaeological excavations in Jerusalem. From Nehemiah 3:8 we learn that Hezekiah's wall was named, appropriately, the Broad Wall.

The revival of the material culture of urban Judah in Iron IIC should be understood in connection with the restoration of the Judean kingdom, first in the latter years of Manasseh but especially under Josiah. The distribution of rosette seal impressions on storage jar handles in the late seventh century attests to a centralized system of distribution and taxation similar to that which was instituted by Hezekiah a century earlier (cf. the LMLK seal impressions). Such policies were wholly consistent with Josiah's centralization of Judean religious practices in Jerusalem. Enough Judean-style pottery has been found in northern sites to indicate trade connections if not an intentional attempt to incorporate former Israelite centers into the revived kingdom of Judah following the Assyrian withdrawal from the area (cf. 2 Kgs 23:19; 2 Chron 34:6).

At the same time, a whole host of religious objects associated with foreign deities have been found throughout Judah, especially in Jerusalem, in Iron IIC. These give material shape to the descriptions of, and invectives against, the worship of Baal and Asherah recorded by the biblical writers (e.g., 2 Kgs 23:4–20; 2 Chron 33:18–19; 34:3–7; Jer 3:9; 7:16–34; 10:1–10). The temple that was constructed within the confines of the Judean fortress at Arad in the tenth century B.C. was finally destroyed ("put out of use" seems to be more consistent with the archaeological record) in the late seventh century, prior to the fort's final destruction a few decades later. This seems to have been due to the reforms of Josiah. That the Holy of Holies in the Arad temple included two standing stones and two incense altars suggests that it served devotees of multiple deities (inscriptions from Arad and Kuntillet 'Ajrud mention both YHWH and Asherah; cf. 2 Kgs 23:6).

The spread of Edomite pottery northwestward from Edom into the southern Negev Highlands and the Negev basins in the late seventh and early sixth centuries B.C. indicates a change in demographics and political control in the area at the end of Iron IIC. Destruction layers at sites throughout Judah, especially at Lachish and, this time, also at Jerusalem, give witness to the campaigns of Nebuchadnezzar. The Lachish letters, ostraca found in the gate of Lachish Level II, record "in the field" details related to Judah's response to the Babylonian advance. One letter, number 4, speaks in desperation of fire signals which can no longer be seen from Azekah, indicating that the city must have just fallen to the Babylonians. Jeremiah 34:7, recording an event that happened shortly before, notes that Azekah and Lachish were the last cities standing outside of Jerusalem. The area of Jerusalem's governmental district, including rooms that housed its archives, saw particularly fierce fighting attested by a thick burn layer interspersed with Babylonian and Judean arrowheads (2 Kgs 25:8–10; 2 Chron 36:19; Jer 52:13–14).

# The Babylonian and Persian Periods (586–331 B.C.)

**Basic Characteristics.** Archaeologists disagree as to whether the short Babylonian Period meets enough criteria to be considered a separate period in the archaeological record in the southern Levant, and if not, if it is better merged with the Iron Age or the Persian Period.[56] There is an overall continuity of material culture, including building and pottery traditions, in Judah from the late seventh century (the end of Iron IIC) until the mid-fifth century B.C., well into the Persian Period. It is true that the destructions of Lachish, Jerusalem and other cities of Judah in 586 B.C. mark the

### MAIN SITES OF THE BABYLONIAN AND PERSIAN PERIODS IN THE SOUTHERN LEVANT

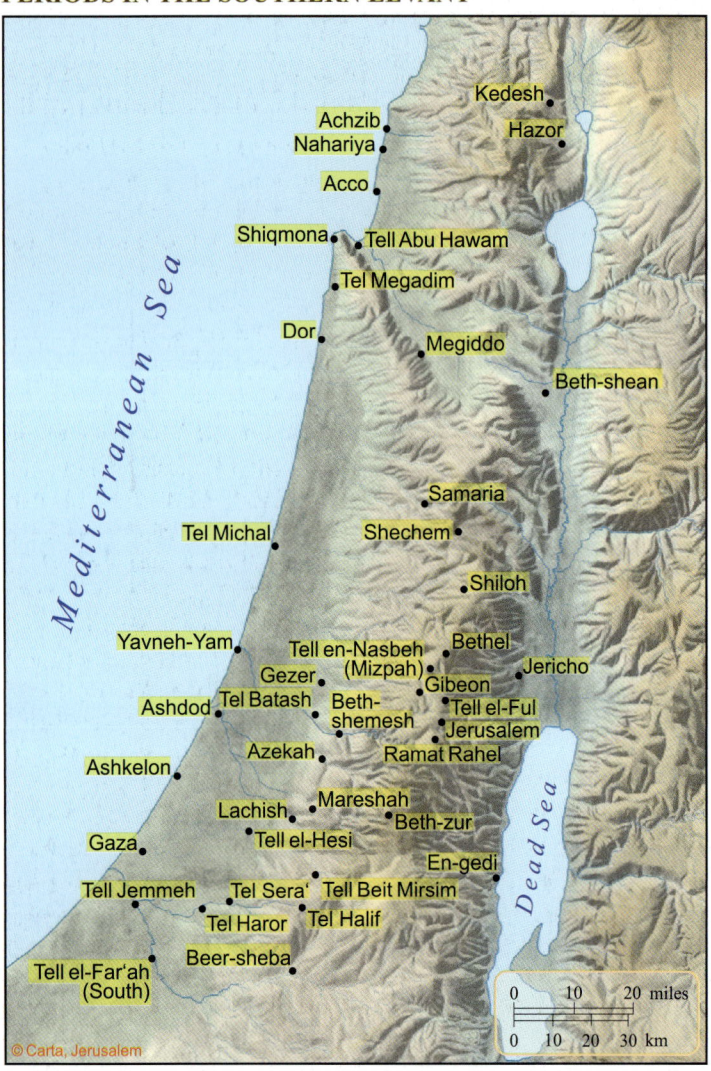

*Limestone head of Tyche, Persian Period, imported to Dor from Cyprus* (courtesy of Ephraim Stern; NEAEHL). *Tyche was the Greek goddess who presided over the fortunes or fate of a Hellenistic city. The job description guaranteed her reverence throughout the ancient world.*

The first significant change in material culture in the southern Levant following the conquest of Judah by Babylon happened only in the mid-fifth century B.C., after the Persian wars in the Aegean had ended. It was then that the Persian kings were able to consolidate their control in the Levant in order to hold onto whatever they could farther west, prompting a brisk rise in Mediterranean trade. For this reason, we must see the traditional division of distinct Babylonian (586–539 B.C.) and Persian (539–331 B.C.) periods as reflecting strictly historical rather than archaeological criteria, marked not by sharp changes in material culture but by the conquests of Nebuchadnezzar (586 B.C.), Cyrus II (539 B.C.) and Alexander the Great (331 B.C.).

This is not to say that the Babylonian Period is invisible in the archaeological record. During the decades following Nebuchadnezzar's conquest of Judah but also in the early Persian Period there was a sharp decline in urban life throughout the southern Levant, combined with an increase in the number of smaller, rural and village sites. This phenomenon can be considered a cultural gap[57] in the sense that the center of gravity of settlement in Judah moved from traditional centers to the rural periphery. Most sites in the Judean hills and the Shephelah were destroyed and not resettled until the mid-Persian Period (e.g., Lachish, Tell Beit Mirsim and Tel Batash). On the other hand, there is evidence of a continuation of settlement at some hill country sites north of Jerusalem (Tell en-Naṣbeh, Tell el-Ful, Gibeon and Bethel), in the hills north of Beth-zur and at Beth-shemesh. Areas farther north that had previously been destroyed and resettled by Assyria passed into Babylonian control without significant change. Babylonian-era pottery in the region shows only small innovations from Iron IIC forms: the disappearance of burnishing and the addition of incised wedge decorations on kraters and jars.

The Babylonian Period is known in Jerusalem mostly from tombs, which stylistically are of the same type as those used in Iron IIC (squared rooms lined on three sides by benches for the bodies, with a repository for bones beneath). Chief among these are the Ketef Hinnom tombs to the southwest of the city. Of them, one was found to be intact. It yielded a pottery assemblage dating from the late seventh to the early fifth centuries B.C., and rich remains such as fine jewelry. Of special note are two silver plaques (amulets) found in the tomb, each of which contains a portion of the blessing of Aaron recorded in Numbers 6:24–26. The Ketef Hinnom tombs indicate that well-to-do families still lived in Jerusalem during the Babylonian Period.

In the Persian Period the lands of Judah and Israel became

Babylonian takeover of the region. Yet archaeological evidence of imperial construction projects, including fortresses, that would signal a change of material culture with Nebuchadnezzar's conquests in the late seventh and early sixth centuries B.C. is lacking everywhere in the Babylonian Empire, including the southern Levant. Moreover, when the Persian king Cyrus II conquered Babylon and inherited its empire in 539 B.C., no destruction layers mark this as the beginning of another new period in the land either. It seems as though the Persian takeover was administrative rather than military in nature, keeping the urban and economic structures of the southern Levant intact to aid Persian moves into Egypt. Persia's wars of conquest under Darius I, Xerxes and Artaxerxes I took place farther west, in Egypt, Anatolia and the Aegean, and it is there rather than in Judah that destruction layers related to the Persian conquest should be sought.

part of the satrapy (province) Beyond the River (*eber nāri*, the Levant west of the Euphrates). Each satrapy was divided into smaller districts or provinces (cf. Esther 1:1), with the districts of the southern Levant largely maintaining the same integrity as the regional divisions of Iron II (Judah, Samaria, Galilee, Ammon, Moab, and the southern Philistine and northern Phoenician coasts). The exception is Idumea, a new political region which included the Negev, the southern Judean hills and the southern Shephelah. The southern Levant in particular was a crucial area for the Persians, who needed functioning centers to supply their war efforts against Egypt, and a line of ports to bridge the world of the ancient Near East with the rising world of the Mediterranean. It is these ports that started to give the material culture of the Levant a truly international character in the Persian Period.

Archaeological evidence for Persian control is most apparent in the latter half of the period, after the mid-fifth century B.C., when the pottery assemblage becomes more distinct. Persian-era pottery is characterized by an increase in finely made Greek vessels, particularly Attic ware, large vessels for domestic use fired with black glaze and decorated with realistic human figures portrayed in beige or red. Hardly any pottery made in Persia itself has been found in the southern Levant, and what is, is not well made. The Persians much preferred to work in metals (including gold), a craft that they perfected. Phoenician pottery of the period was yellowish-green in color rather than tan-red as in the Iron Age, and found prominently at sites along the coast and in the Galilee hills. Many other small objects found in the southern Levant attest to the internationalism of the age: stone statues in Cypriot and Greek styles, clay figurines of all types exhibiting Egyptian, Persian, Greek and Phoenician influences, and coins. Coins, which first appeared in the ancient world in western Asia Minor (Sardis) in the seventh century B.C., signaled a change from a barter to a monetary economy. This opened new opportunities for trade, especially by sea. Coins of all kinds have been found in the southern Levant, becoming common only at the very end of the Persian Period. These include gold Persian *darics* and coins from Greece. Most of the commerce in the eastern Mediterranean used coins minted on the Athenian standard and many were circulated via the ports lining the coast, though surprisingly only a very few have been found at sites south of Phoenicia in the Persian Period. "Small change" coins minted from silver and bronze at Tyre and Sidon, however, were particularly common throughout the region. Local coins were struck at Gaza, Ashkelon, Samaria and Jerusalem. Of special note are coins struck

*Jar handle (left) and coin (below) stamped with* yhd, *the Persian province Yehud.* (NEAEHL)

in Jerusalem with the designation *yhd*, for Yehud, the Persian name of the district of Judah. These typically bore a falcon and a lily.

Fortresses built to solidify Persian control of the southern Levant in the late fifth and fourth centuries B.C. tended to be similar to fortresses constructed by the Assyrians in the seventh century, with an inner courtyard surrounded by rooms forming a casemate wall. Often granaries were found nearby. These appear on former Iron II sites throughout the country, though mostly in the southern regions facing Egypt. They included Lachish, Mareshah and Beer-sheba in outer Idumea, as well as Tell el-Kheleifeh, Kadesh-barnea and Meẓad Ḥazeva to the south. Similar sites in Philistia include Tell Jemmeh, Tel Seraʻ, Tel Haror (Gerar), Tell el-Ḥesi, Tell el-Farʻah South and Tel Ḥalif. Significantly, over two hundred sites of all kinds with Persian material remains have been found scattered across the northern Sinai between Gaza and the Suez Canal. These include towns, villages, forts, cemeteries and seasonal encampments, and attest to active Persian efforts to subdue Egypt and benefit from the trade between it, Arabia and the Mediterranean. In the north, virtually all of the main Iron II sites of Samaria and Galilee also show fortified Persian remains, including Shechem, Megiddo, Hazor and Kedesh. In Transjordan most of the Persian forts were found in the vicinity of Ammon, the Moabite Plain (*Mishor*) to the south, and the central Jordan Valley.

The coast from Phoenicia to Ashkelon, together with the large northern inland valleys, was the most densely settled part of the southern Levant during the Persian Period. From the archaeological record it appears to have been generally quite prosperous. This was no doubt due to active commercial ties with the Aegean, and articles of Greek manufacture have been found at every site in the region. To facilitate Mediterranean trade, Acco moved from the mouth of the Naʻaman River to the bay of the current Crusader city. The first breakwater for the new port at Acco was built in the Persian Period, built with header ashlars on a pebble base like the breakwaters of Tyre and Sidon. Typical Phoenician large-building architecture had walls constructed of header-stretcher ashlar piers with fieldstone fills between (Tyre, Acco, Megiddo, Achzib, Tell Abu Hawam, Tel Michal and Yavneh-Yam). This style was already common in Iron II and continued well into the Hellenistic Period. The earliest example of the Hippodamian town plan has been found at Dor (in the late sixth century), with elements of the plan dating to later in the Persian Period found at Shiqmona, Tel Megadim, Acco, Nahariya, Tell Abu Hawam, Ashkelon and Ashdod. This style of urban planning, which was to become common in the Hellenistic and Roman periods, was characterized by streets laid out in a grid pattern which divided the town into specific areas (*insula*) based on various civic functions

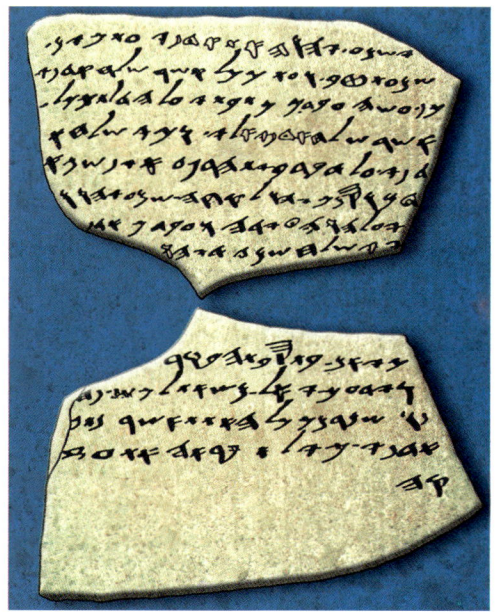

*Lachish letter no. 4 from level II of the tel, marking the end of the Judean Kingdom by the Babylonian conquest.* (Ada Yardeni)

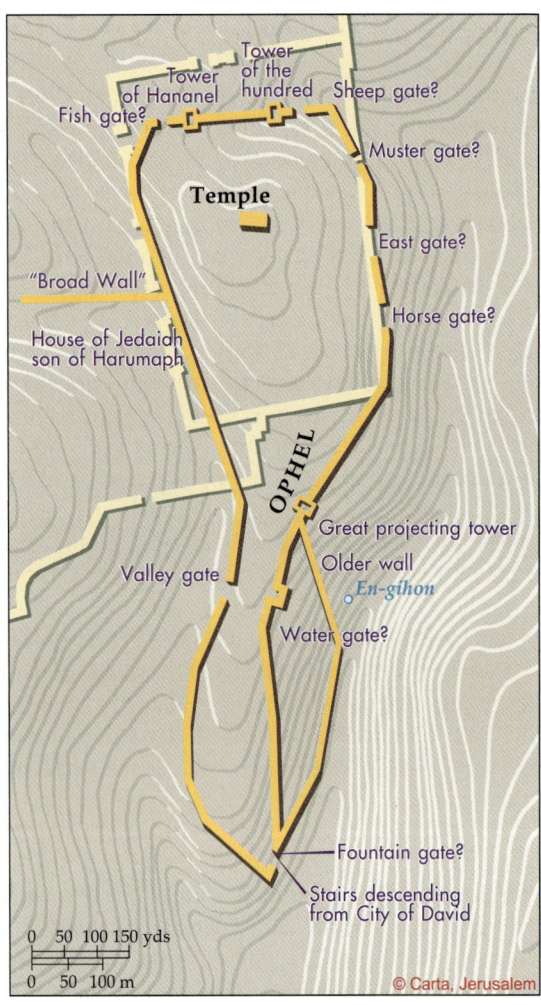

**JERUSALEM IN THE TIME OF NEHEMIAH** *(indicating that the city wall circled the eastern hill, a position held by some but not all scholars)*

(residential, commercial, industrial, cultic and sport).

Down in Yehud (Judah), handles of storage jars stamped with the designation *yhd* have been found at sites from Mizpeh to Jericho and En-gedi in the east, over to Gezer in the west. This distribution marks the borders of the district Yehud, the Persian Period territorial remnant of the Iron Age kingdom of Judah. Names of several of the governors of Yehud are known from various finds: Bagoas (mentioned in Elephantine Papyri dating to the end of the fifth century B.C.), Jehoezer and Aḥzai (from seal impressions at Ramat Raḥel), and Yeḥezkiah whose name has been found on a *yhd* coin from Beth-zur dating to the fourth century. To these can be added Nehemiah (Neh 5:14). Only a very few pieces of Persian era pottery have been found on Jerusalem's western hill, suggesting that settlement in the old Judean capital fell back to the city's original eastern (City of David) hill, where Persian pottery and bullae are more commonly found. More difficult is the question of how much of Jerusalem was walled, a matter which has not been solved by archaeology because of the lack of structural remains that can be securely dated to the Persian Period.[58] By the end of the Persian Period, however, Jerusalem had grown to become by far the major urban center in the hills, though its material culture lagged behind that of the more prosperous cities on the coast.

Further afield, archaeological evidence for Jews in Babylon is scarce. Jews can be identified in economic texts found in excavations in southern Babylonia that contain personal names ending in the -*yhw* suffix. The largest corpus of information comes from the cuneiform Murashu archive, which records the business activities of a Jewish banking family in the second half of the fifth century B.C.[59] The Elephantine texts from Upper Egypt (Aswan) attest to a viable Jewish community there in the fifth century. The texts even mention a Jewish temple serving the Egyptian community, foundation remains of which have been found in excavation on the southern end of Elephantine island at Aswan near the first cataract of the Nile.[60]

**Biblical Connections.** The Babylonian and early Persian Periods correspond to the Exilic and Post-Exilic periods of biblical history (Gedaliah through Ezra–Nehemiah). Together they coincide with a 150-year transitional period in the archaeological record between the classic material culture of Iron IIC and the classic material culture of the Persian Period, which appears only after the mid-fifth century B.C.

The Babylonians exiled only the upper classes of Judah, allowing the poorer people to remain in their land (2 Kgs 25:12; Jer 39:9–10; 52:15–16). It was, according to the prophet Zechariah, "a day of small things" (Zech 4:10). Here the archaeological record is consistent with the biblical account in that we would not expect to see a noticeable change in material culture related to basic things of livelihood or urban architecture. Continued settlement at Tell en-Naṣbeh and at central Benjamin sites in its vicinity corresponds with the biblical account of Mizpeh becoming the Babylonian capital in place of Jerusalem (2 Kgs 25:23–25). The Ketef Hinnom tomb finds suggest that some of the wealthy families of Jerusalem remained, though there is no archaeological evidence that they attempted to reconstitute an urban Judean presence in the land. The amulets found in one of the Ketef Hinnom tombs offer the earliest citation of texts found in the Bible (Num 6:24–26). It is also the earliest confessional statement about the LORD God of Israel, finding parallels in biblical texts of the Post-Exilic Period (Neh 1:5; Dan 9:4).

The Cyrus Cylinder, a cuneiform text found in the ruins of Babylon by which Cyrus II justified his rule over Babylon by declaring himself to be the choice of the city's national god, Marduk, speaks of the king's decision to "resettle in their sacred cities" the deities of the lands previously conquered by Nebuchadnezzar.[61] The writer of Chronicles understood Cyrus' decree as giving official permission for the exiled Judeans to return to Jerusalem and rebuild the Temple (2 Chron 36:22–23). The name of the large province of which Yehud and its neighbors were composite parts, Beyond the River, resonated with the writers of Ezra and Nehemiah in that it reflected the maximal extent of the borders of the Solomonic kingdom (1 Kgs 4:21; cf. Ezra 4:10–11; 8:36, Neh 2:7).

Nehemiah, the governor of Yehud (Neh 5:14), organized an effort to rebuild the walls of Jerusalem in the mid-fifth century, at the time that the Persians were settling into the Levant for the long haul. The distribution of *yhd* jar handle stamps found in excavation (at Jerusalem, Ramat Raḥel, el-Azariya, Jericho, En-gedi, Mizpah, Azekah and Gezer) corresponds to the territorial extent of the region of Yehud from which workmen came to rebuild the city wall (Nehemiah 3). The description of the wall in Nehemiah 2–3 offers the most detailed picture of a city wall in any text from the ancient world, prompting archaeologists and historians alike to try to identify at least something of its remains. Nehemiah's work on the wall of Jerusalem, which was completed hastily in the course of just 52 days (Neh 6:15; cf. 4:3), was certainly a repair of the Iron II walls rather than completely new construction. Because of the large number of city gates and wall towers mentioned in Nehemiah's description, it is likely on textual grounds alone that Nehemiah repaired the wall that encircled the entirety of Jerusalem rather than just the smaller eastern (City of David) hill. The ceramic evidence suggests that the population of post-exilic Jerusalem, however, was concentrated in the older, eastern part of the city, which is consistent with Nehemiah's description that while Jerusalem was large, the people within were few (Neh 7:4; 11:1–2).

# The Hellenistic (331–142 B.C.) and Hasmonean Periods (142–63 B.C.)

**Basic Characteristics.** When Alexander the Great reached the land of ancient Israel in 331 B.C. on his eastward march to conquer the known world, he put a formal political stamp on the penetration of Hellenistic culture that was already flowing into the region. With the rule of his successors in Judea, first the Ptolemies of Egypt (301–198 B.C.) but especially the Seleucids based in Syrian Antioch (198–142 B.C.), the flood tide of Greek material culture and thought inundated the land. Affects are seen in architecture, city planning, pottery, tools and art, but also in literature, philosophy and religion. In response, a revival of Jewish nationalism under

### MAIN HELLENISTIC AND HASMONEAN SITES IN THE SOUTHERN LEVANT

the Hasmoneans (the Maccabees) led to an independent Jewish state in 142 B.C. Sequences of abandonment and resettlement at sites throughout the land attest to epic battles between the powers, though it is difficult to discern an overall pattern in the destruction layers. With few exceptions, this makes it difficult to match any given destruction with any particular historic event. What is clear is that the southern Levant was a frontier for all things Hellenism, whether they be political or cultural in nature. It was here, under the focused energy of the Hasmonean kingdom, that material forms that were otherwise classically Jewish, classically Hellenistic or even classically Egyptian melded and mixed in some very creative ways.

The overall picture of the early Hellenistic Period, the late fourth through third centuries B.C., is one which shows general continuity with settlement patterns of the late Persian Period. At nearly every site on the coast that preserves archaeological evidence of settlement in the fifth and fourth centuries B.C., there are clear indications of continued settlement well into the third. In contrast to the coast but also consistent with the archaeological picture of the previous century, there were but few urban centers in the inland hills of the southern Levant in the Hellenistic Period. Each served an agricultural economy that was not well connected to Mediterranean trade. Important aspects of material culture, too, show continuity with the Persian Period. Building styles and artifactual remains from the decades following Alexander's conquest are virtually identical with those from the decades before. From an abundance of stamped amphora we can conclude that the export of local wheat, wine and purple dye from coastal Levantine sites continued unabated, as did the import of fine wines, honey, oil and expensive vessels and utensils from many sites in the Aegean and Italy. Clear burn layers at coastal cities that can be attributed to the conquests of Alexander or his successors are relatively rare (Tyre, Dor and Ashkelon). All of this indicates that the traditional break between the Persian and Hellenistic periods was historical rather than archaeological in nature, and that Alexander's conquest, for all its military effectiveness, did not interrupt but rather spurred opportunities for international trade.

Archaeological evidence reveals the prosperity of coastal sites during the Hellenistic Period. Ashkelon, Tel Mor (the port of Ashdod) and Dor (renamed Dora to give the city a Greek accent) had large, sumptuous villas. The city wall of Dor was rebuilt with large ashlars set headers-out, helping to make the city "a fortress difficult to take" (*Ant.* 13.223). This technique, typical at Greek sites, is also seen at other places in the southern Levant in the

*Seven courses of stones from the Hasmonean period fit snugly between two piers of bedrock, forming the foundation of a tower in the western city wall of Jerusalem in the 2nd century B.C. The wall was well located. Stones from the Medieval period (center) and the Ottoman Turkish period (top) show that a tower also stood here in the centuries following, up to today.*

*Remains of a strong tower dating to the Hellenistic Period can be seen at Samaria, site of the Israelite capital during the Iron Age. The tower was constructed with three rings of ashlar blocks, all slightly wedge-shaped and set headers-out. When attacked by a battering ram, the stones of the tower would only tighten together.*

Hellenistic Period (e.g., Mareshah and Samaria). Ship-building installations near the harbor of Dor tied the city's economy to Phoenicia (sufficient timber for the industry was available on Mount Carmel). Excavations at both Dor and Tel Mor have uncovered installations for manufacturing purple dye from murex shells. The residents of Acco, who had already moved from the tel to the natural promontory at the edge of the sea, strengthened their breakwater and port. Acco was renamed Ptolemais early in the third century B.C., the only coastal city given a completely new, Hellenized name. Fittingly, Ptolemais served as an important Levantine launch pad for the Ptolemaic dynasty's maritime trade.

In the south, Gaza grew in importance as a warehousing center at the expense of other southern cities. Tell Jemmeh, Tel Nagila and Tell el-Ḥesi were all abandoned after the fourth century B.C. At the same time, a new line of settlements appeared in the Negev highlands connecting Gaza with the Arabian Peninsula. These include Nessana, Elusa, Avdat and Mo'a, together marking a spice route that was operated by the Nabateans, a people group that appears in historic documents for the first time in the late fourth century B.C.[62] The Zenon papyri, found in Faiyum Egypt, attest to wheat, oil, wine, spices and slaves moving to Egypt via Gaza in the mid-third century B.C. The papyri also mention that goods moving through Phoenician ports were subject to tax rates of up to fifty percent. When one considers the archaeological evidence for prosperity at sites throughout the coast in the Hellenistic Period in spite of a voluminous tax rate, the overall picture of a viable, growing economy in the region is undeniable.

Inland, in Idumea (the Shephelah), Mareshah grew into a large and wealthy market town built on the Hippodamian town plan with headers-out architecture, equal in sophistication to Ashkelon and Dor. Though Ptolemy I strongly fortified the tel to serve as the city's acropolis (c. 300 B.C.), most of the settlement at Mareshah (Marisa) moved to the lower, level ground surrounding its base, as was typical in the Hellenistic Period. Best preserved at Mareshah today are numerous underground installations lying west and south

**PLAN OF HELLENISTIC MARESHAH/MARISA**

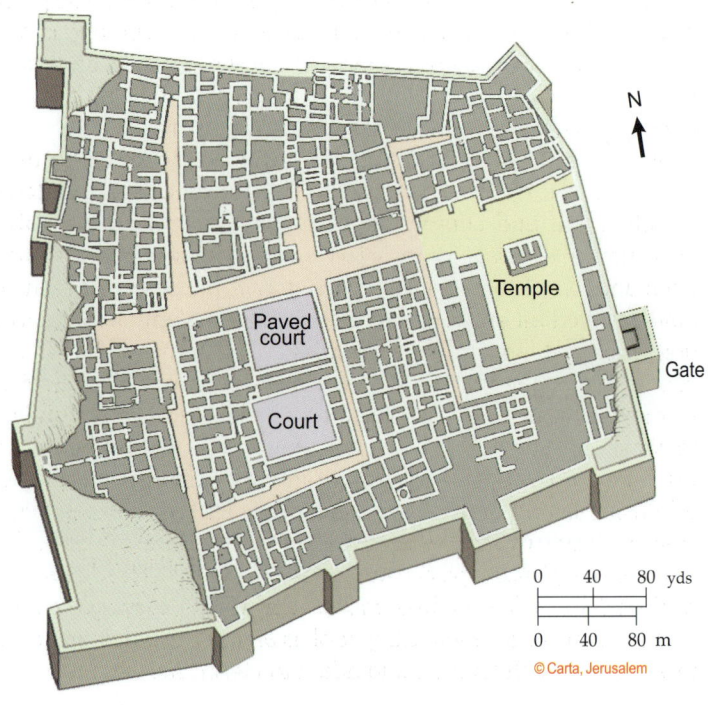

*The central burial hall in tomb 1 (the Sidonian tomb) at Mareshah, Hellenistic Period, restored. This was the family tomb of Apollophanes, apparent head of the Sidonian community in the city.*

*A lion and her cub appear in bold relief on the upper storey of the west side of the palace-fortress Qasr el-Abd at 'Iraq al-Amir. The building belonged to Hyrcanus, grandson of Tobias, an ambitious but thwarted power-broker who fled Jerusalem for the safety of western Gilead in the early second century B.C. (Ant. 12.228–234).*

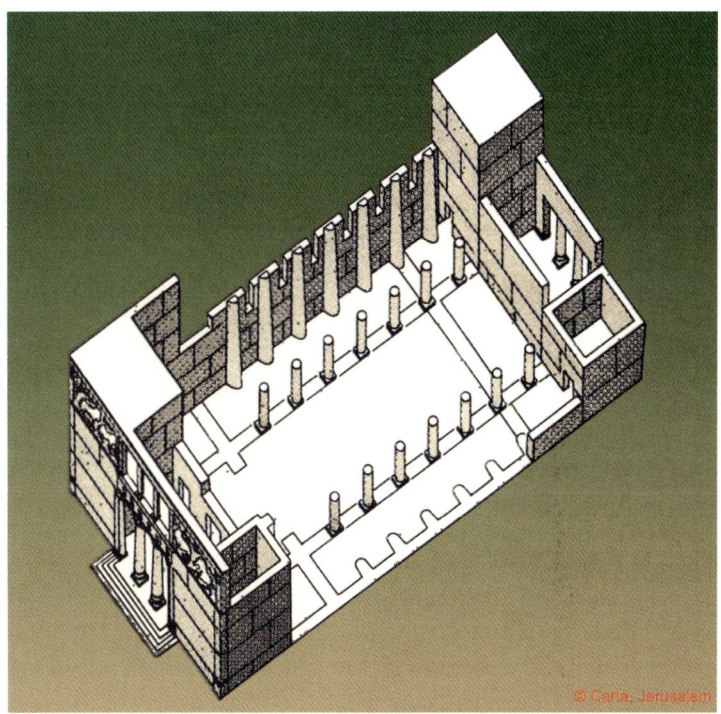

*(right) Reconstruction of the palace-fortress at 'Iraq al-Amir.*

of the tel, including a huge columbarium for raising pigeons and industrial shops for producing olive oil. What is left of the houses above ground shows Mediterranean influence in architecture and style. Most striking at Mareshah, though, are two tombs painted with brilliant images of real and imaginary animals and people, all decorated in a Phoenician style (one of the tombs belonged to a native of Sidon).

The hill country of Judah remained largely unsettled well into the third century B.C., with Jerusalem the only large city in the area. Its material culture was primarily locally made rather than imported. There is in fact little evidence that international trade reached the central hills of the southern Levant until the Hasmonean Period, hence there was little for the Ptolemaic overlords to tax. Taxes instead seem to have been paid annually rather than on a per instance basis, as evidenced by storage jars that were stamped *yhd* (a holdover from Persian administration) as well as *yrslm* (for Jerusalem, probably designating a Temple tax). All in all, we know less of Jerusalem archaeologically during the early Hellenistic Period than we know of it during any other period since MB II.

A similar picture attains for the hills north of Jerusalem. Shechem and Samaria were the only sizable settlements in what used to be heartland of the northern kingdom of Israel during the third century B.C. There was active building at Shechem from the fourth century, probably related to an emerging Samaritan community in the region. The summit of Mount Gerizim, standing above Shechem to the south, was encircled by a wall in the mid-third century, enclosing well-built houses and a large structure that was, apparently, the Samaritan temple. Samaria city was destroyed by Alexander, then rebuilt with a perimeter wall fortified by round, headers-out towers, the ashlars of which were decorated with wide, smooth margins and a rough, raised boss. This decoration style would become typical of late Hellenistic (Hasmonean) construction.

Archaeological evidence suggests that settlement was also not very heavy in Galilee, with only a few sites showing occupation in the third century B.C. (Tell Keisan and Tel Qiri at the western end of the Jezreel Valley; Kinneret and Philoteria/Beth Yeraḥ on the Sea of Galilee). In a pattern that was repeated in the Roman Period, the western end of the Jezreel Valley became royal land farmed for the king (the Ptolemies). There is no archaeological evidence of trade or industry in the area to further bolster the economy.

Archaeological evidence from Tel Anafa in the northern Hula basin shows the same pattern—small, unsophisticated agricultural sites not connected to the trade patterns of the coast. Poorly made offering vessels show that Banias was already being used as a local cult site in the third century B.C., prior to erection of the buildings associated with the cult of Pan. A small pagan shrine consisting of a raised platform decorated with frescoes with beautifully frescoed walls was built in the Hellenistic Period at Khirbet Omrit, just to the south of Banias.

The only exception to this pattern of rather rudimentary settlement in the Galilee during the Hellenistic Period is Beth-shean, which was reestablished as Scythopolis sometime in the late third century B.C. As with similarly-situated Hellenistic cities of the southern Levant, the settlement of Scythopolis slid to the bottom of the tel of Beth-shean. Unlike other cities in the Jezreel Valley system, the archaeological evidence at Scythopolis shows evidence of the kind of cosmopolitan wealth that characterized the coast. Farther east, in Transjordan, the old Ammonite capital, Rabbah, was re-founded in the mid-third century as Philadelphia by Ptolemy II Philadelphus, evidenced in part by headers-out ashlar walls. Scythopolis and Philadelphia became the launch pad for what would become a strong urban Greek *polis* presence in the territory that lay between them, referred to in Roman times as the Decapolis.

When the southern Levant fell to the Seleucid king Antiochus III in a series of battles between 201 and 198 B.C., the overall patterns of settlement and commerce in the region—with the notable exception of Jerusalem—remained largely the same as they had been under the Ptolemies and Persians. Still, the Seleucids seem to have fostered an environment that favored Hellenistic forms to a greater extend than did the Ptolemies. The first half of the second century B.C. is when we first see clear evidence in the archaeological record of classical Greek architecture in Judea and the surrounding regions. The Doric Order is seen in Jerusalem and Shechem, and the Ionic Order, a development from the proto-Ionic capitals of Iron II Judah and Israel, also in Jerusalem. Tel Anafa turned into a Hellenistic city with the earliest evidence of mosaics in the land. The remains of a pleasure palace at 'Iraq al-Amir in the Gilead hills west of Philadelphia (Rabbath-ammon), replete with carvings of lions and surrounded by a reflecting pool, is an early example of how a prominent Jewish family could adapt to Hellenistic lifestyles.

## JERUSALEM IN THE HASMONEAN PERIOD

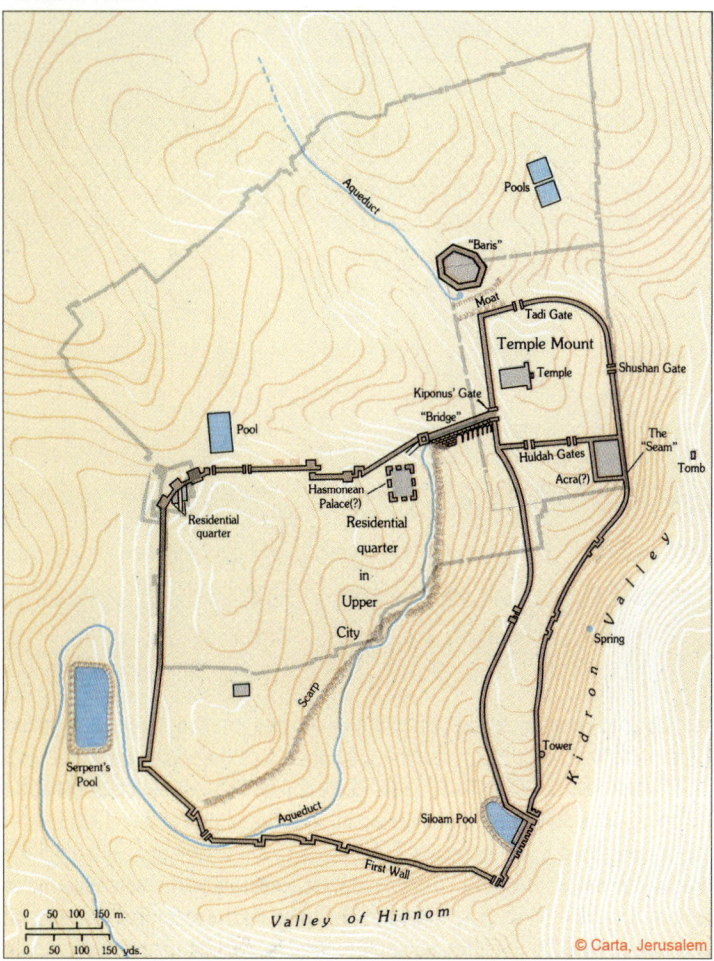

The city of Jerusalem in particular showed increased material prosperity in the decades leading up to and following the Seleucid takeover of the region. In the first major building projects since the days of Nehemiah, the city's fortifications, especially those around the Temple complex, were improved. A section of the eastern retaining wall of the Temple Mount north of the so-called "straight joint" that is composed of ashlars with wide margins and a rough boss laid in a header-stretcher pattern may have been constructed during the days of the high priesthood of Simon, as noted in Sirach 50:1–3. A large number of stamped Rhodian amphora handles found in the City of David section of Jerusalem attests to increased commercial activities with the Aegean. An increase in the number of small finds on Jerusalem's western hill suggests that settlement was also growing there. Antiochus IV Epiphanes (175–164 B.C.) constructed a fortified citadel near the Temple Mount in Jerusalem (the Akra; 1 Macc 1:33; *Ant.* 12.252), the location of which has been the object of much speculation though nothing has been found of it archaeologically.

The well-publicized activities of Antiochus IV to turn Jerusalem into a center of Hellenism led the Jews to revolt in 167 B.C. For the next 25 years, until the Seleucids recognized an independent Jewish (Hasmonean) state in Judea in 142 B.C., a Jewish army led by the Maccabees engaged Seleucid forces in a number of battles and skirmishes in the Judean hills. This frantic and bloody struggle is not as well represented in the archaeological record as might be expected. Traces of wall construction at Bethel and Gezer may reflect the fortification of these sites by the Seleucid general Bacchides. In turn, evidence of new fortifications at Beth-zur in the mid-second century may be related to the actions of a Jewish garrison there. The rest of the country shows no changes of substance in the archaeological record, suggesting that for the most part conditions in the area remained stable. Some cities on the coast (Ashdod and Strato's Tower) even expanded.

The overall picture provided by archaeology for the century of Hasmonean control in the southern Levant attests to a period of consolidation and growth rather than one of division and attack as the historical sources (Josephus and the books of Maccabees) might otherwise indicate. There is much more evidence of construction and fortification than there is for destruction layers throughout the region. Prosperity is especially evident on the coast, in the region of Banias where the Pan cult had become established in the far north, and in Jerusalem. There was a sharp increase in the number of sites in and adjacent to the hills of Judea and Samaria as the Hasmonean kingdom took root. These include sites that seem to have been both agricultural villages and strategic outposts. It is also in the hill country that most of the relevant destruction layers in the second half of the second century B.C. can be found, at Beth-zur, Gezer, Mareshah, Shechem, Mount Gerizim and Dothan. All are evidence that the Hasmoneans under Jonathan and John Hyrcanus seem to have cleaned house in order to establish the heartland of their kingdom in the hills that had been controlled by Israel and Judah in the Iron Age. There is also archaeological evidence of Hyrcanus' campaign on the southern coast, with destruction layers at Ashdod and Yavneh-Yam (Jamnia). On the other hand, neither Hyrcanus' campaign in Transjordan (*Ant.* 13.254–255) nor that of Aristobulus in Iturea (*Ant.* 13.318) can be verified archaeologically. As the Hasmoneans were building and consolidating their state, their neighbors (the Nabateans and Itureans as well as Ascalon, Ptolemais, Tyre and Sidon) were doing the same, having also purchased or declared their independence from the Seleucids.

The city of Jerusalem began to take on large, elegant portions in the Hasmonean Period. The Hasmonean kings Jonathan, Simon and Alexander Jannaeus all worked on rebuilding the walls of Jerusalem, with Jannaeus finishing the wall around the city's western hill (1 Macc 10:10–11; 13:10). This is what Josephus called the First Wall (*War* 5.142–145). It can be seen in several places as the wide margin, rough boss ashlars that form the lower courses of towers and wall segments that support the current city wall of Jerusalem, though it is not possible to identify any specific

*Coins of Antiochus IV Epiphanes (left) and Alexander Jannaeus (below). One popular coin minted by Jannaeus depicted an eight-pointed star interspersed with Hebrew letters reading "Yehonatan the king" on one side, with an anchor and Greek inscription "of King Alexander" on the other.*

part with the efforts of any specific Hasmonean king. Everywhere there has been excavation on the western hill, late Hellenistic and Hasmonean remains are found directly on remains from the end of Iron II. Hasmonean-era building remains have been found in the area of Herod's Palace (in today's Armenian Quarter inside Jaffa Gate), suggesting that the Hasmonean Palace was likely in the same area. From it, a bridge led over the central (Tyropoean) valley to the Temple Mount. Part of this can still be seen on el-Wad street just north of the Western Wall plaza. Remains of a large tower on the crest of the eastern slope of the City of David just south of the Iron I stepped stone revetment wall shows that the oldest part of the city was also fortified by the Hasmoneans. The Hasmonean kings also seem to have been the first to construct an aqueduct to bring water to Jerusalem from the Hebron hills, portions of which can still be traced along the contour of the hills between. The earliest construction at the so-called Solomon's Pools south of Bethlehem, three huge reservoirs used to store water prior to its run to Jerusalem, may date to the Hasmonean Period.

By the end of the second century B.C. there is material evidence of conspicuous wealth among the elite of Jerusalem. This is seen partly by outwardly elaborate family tombs which combine Greek and Egyptian architectural elements in ways that bent the rules of classic forms. One example is the tomb which may have belonged to the family of the high priest Jason (2 Macc 4:10–13; cf. 1 Macc 13:27–29) located in the Rehavia neighborhood of modern west Jerusalem. Jason's Tomb has a pyramid roof, a single Doric column in its façade and charcoal drawings of Mediterranean ships on its interior walls. Another is the tomb of the priestly Hezir family opposite the Temple Mount in the Kidron Valley which has a classic Doric façade. The interior of both were designed with loculi (*kochim*) designed to hold limestone ossuaries, boxes for the bones of the deceased. Ossuary burials were typical of the first century B.C. and first century A.D. and seem to indicate an emphasis on individual afterlife. Other aspects of the material culture of Hasmonean Jerusalem seem to indicate a return to distinctively Jewish forms, perhaps due to religious scruples or the result of altered networks of trade. These include a noticeable increase in the number of ritual immersion baths (*miqva'ot*), the disappearance of Rhodian jar handles, and pottery that was made locally rather than imported or in Greek styles. The introduction of Eastern Terra Sigillata ware (very fine vessels with a thick, bright red-orange slip) manufactured in Phoenicia became popular throughout the southern coastal cities, the Negev (e.g., Nessana and Avdat), Transjordan and Galilee, but not at sites in the hill country of Judea or Samaria, the Hasmonean heartland (that would happen in the Herodian Period).

The same ambivalence between Jewish and Greek forms found in Jerusalem during the Hasmonean Period can also be seen in the material culture of sites throughout the region. Qumran provides one type of example. Here multiple *miqva'ot* within a walled compound attest to utilitarian, separatist intentions of a sect consistent with the community of the Dead Sea Scrolls. The Hasmonean palaces at nearby Jericho, likely built by Alexander Jannaeus, are a good example of the opposite extreme—they include a pool/garden complex, a bathhouse, villas and banquet halls with frescoed walls. Alexander Jannaeus also built or rebuilt Hyrcania, Dok, Alexandrium and Machaerus in the hills lining the Rift to serve as elaborate desert fortresses, treasure houses and prisons (*War* 1.161; *Ant.* 13.417). Jannaeus was the first Hasmonean king to mint coins in great quantity (they are very common in excavations), an indication that he wanted an economy that was independent from, yet tied to that of his neighbors. His coins include inscriptions in both Hebrew and Greek. At the same time, in Idumea and on the coast (with few exceptions, e.g., Ashkelon) signs of Mediterranean

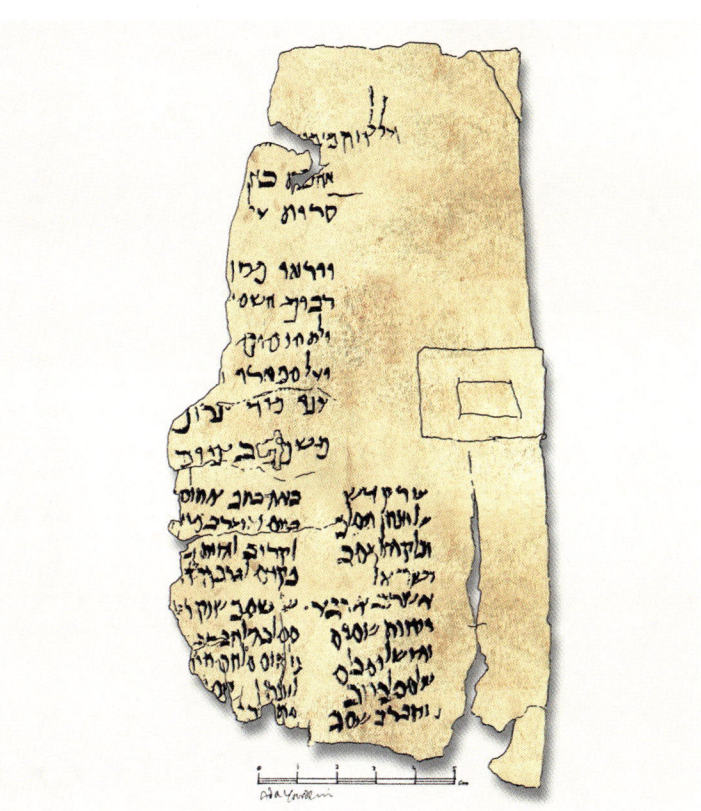

*Liturgical poem in a semi-cursive Hasmonean script from Qumran (4Q448) mentioning Jonathan the King (Alexander Jannaeus).* (Ada Yardeni)

trade diminish in favor of Judean-made vessels and less-elaborate architectural forms. The distribution of these patterns of material culture provides a practical map of Hasmonean control while indicating that it was only the highest echelons of Hasmonean society that enjoyed a steady supply of Greek material comfort.

Toward the end of the first half of the first century B.C. many sites of all kinds throughout the country were destroyed, with a noticeable number abandoned. This widespread destruction is concurrent with the Roman takeover of the region by Pompey in 63 B.C. Surprisingly, though, there is no specific archaeological evidence to confirm the destruction, in whole or in part, of cities that Josephus specifically mentions as having been conquered by Pompey (Jerusalem, Hippus, Scythopolis/Beth-shean, Pella, Dium, Samaria, Marisa/Mareshah, Azotus/Ashdod, Jamnia and Arethusa; *Ant.* 14:58–75).

**Biblical Connections.** Like the Bronze Ages were to the time of the Old Testament, the archaeology of the Hellenistic and Hasmonean Periods are prior to and contextual to the New Testament. The areas of the southern Levant that factored into networks of imperial trade, namely the coastal plain and large inland valleys, benefited the most from the economic forces of Hellenism, while the hilly heartland of the old biblical kingdoms of Israel and especially Judah tended to remain more provincial. One can sense in the rich material culture the challenges as well as the opportunities that would come to face the peoples of the New Testament a few decades later. In broad strokes the available archaeological material confirms the tumultuous narrative accounts of Josephus and the books of Maccabees. Still, there are many instances of destruction layers not found in the archaeological record even though they might be expected from the historical accounts. Because in this case the interface (or lack thereof) of archaeology and text involves texts other than the Bible, it provides a welcome template by which to view similar instances in which the Bible provides the primary historical witness.

# The Early Roman (Herodian) Period (63 B.C.–A.D. 135)

**Basic Characteristics.** The Early Roman Period began with the conquest of Phoenicia and Coele-Syria by Pompey in 63 B.C. and ended with the Roman suppression of the Bar Kochba revolt in A.D. 135. These two centuries are often called the Second Temple Period in reference to Herod the Great's rebuilding of the Jerusalem Temple, even though his was actually the third construction of the building (after Solomon and Zerubbabel). The term Herodian Period is also appropriate for this time because the archaeological remains of the period are dominated by the personality of the Herodian family, this even though the dynasty reigned in one capacity or another only from 37 B.C. to c. A.D. 100, and over a territory with wildly fluctuating borders. Still, Herod the Great provided both the inspiration and the opportunities to put a stamp on the material culture of the southern Levant that has been unparalleled in size, creativity and sheer compunction to today.

## MAIN EARLY ROMAN (HERODIAN) SITES IN THE SOUTHERN LEVANT

Although there is no clear archaeological evidence of Pompey's conquest of Judea in 63 B.C., there is of a follow-up campaign six years later in which the Syrian governor Gabinius destroyed Machaerus to take it out of Hasmonean hands (*Ant.* 14.89). There is also archaeological evidence that Gabinius rebuilt parts of Samaria on the Hippodamian plan (*Ant.* 14.87–88; *War* 1.166). On the other hand, no clear archaeological evidence marks the Parthian invasion of 40 B.C., nor of the conquest of Galilee and Judea by Herod in 37 B.C.

It is only with the establishment of the Herodian dynasty that significant remains of the period can be identified in the archaeological record, including many that corroborate the lavishly written accounts of the time by Josephus. It is not always clear which Herodian architectural elements were constructed by Herod the Great and which should be attributed to his sons, his grandson Agrippa I or his great-grandson Agrippa II. In the end Herod has probably gotten more credit than he should.[63] For instance, we now know that the wall-supporting extension of the Temple Mount platform toward the south and west, built of massive stones sporting classic Herodian margin-and-boss decorations (of which the so-called Robinson's Arch is a part) was not begun until after A.D. 18, over two decades following Herod's death, based on coins found under the lowest course of stones forming the southwestern corner of the wall.

The writings of Josephus give lengthy and elaborate descriptions of Herodian building projects and other aspects of the material culture of the first centuries B.C. and A.D. Additional relevant written material can be found in the New Testament as well as in writings from later periods (e.g., the Mishnah and Talmud). Most scholarly and popular descriptions of the Herodian Period, and of Jerusalem in particular, are based on these literary sources. Even though the sheer amount of archaeologically recoverable material for the period is massive, there is still a large gap between it and the literary sources in terms of data known. In spite of this gap, it is clear that the archaeological evidence by and large substantiates these written accounts. Herod's footprint was so heavy that even before excavations, it was possible to identify his work by visible surface remains (e.g., at Masada, Herodium, Caesarea, Jerusalem and the Cave of Machpelah in Hebron).

Iron Age architecture was first and foremost functional. No one has accused four-room houses or casemate walls of being pretty. By contrast, while Imperial Roman architecture was also functional, it was nearly always beautiful. These are among the most dramatic lasting symbols of Rome and of the personalities of its benefactors and kings. Herod, aptly described as a megalomaniac, meant to impress, and he still does today. By all estimations Herod's building activity took place over the course of just two decades starting sometime after 30 B.C. That he was able to accomplish so much in such a short period of time, and such a high level of craftsmanship, is incredible, and could scarcely be believed on literary grounds alone without the proof found in the reality of the archaeological record. Architectural forms attributed to Herod include huge decorated ashlars; bridges, passageways and aqueducts supported by arches; columns of both the Ionic and Corinthian orders; colorful frescoes, mosaics and floors of *opus sectile* (large stone tiles set in geometric designs); decorated stucco ceilings; baths, pools and gardens; theatres and peristyle courtyards. The work throughout betrays evidence of highly skilled architects and builders trained in Rome.

It is possible to place the building projects of Herod the Great for which there is archaeological evidence into two groups, generally following the chronological order in which they were constructed.[64] The earlier projects likely included the fortresses of Alexandrium, Hyrcania, Cypros and Masada. Several if not all of these were on the site of previous Hasmonean building projects. It seems as though Herod wanted to both incorporate and obliterate the memory of the Jewish dynasty that he replaced. All can be termed "palace fortresses" on the grounds that they incorporated elements of elegant decoration and comfort into structures that enforced Roman imperial might. Sophisticated aqueduct systems transported, then

*Remains of a series of three nested Roman-style temples at Omrit in the northern Huleh Basin give witness to the inroads of classic architecture in the first century A.D. The second of the three seems to have been built by Herod the Great and the outermost, the walls of which are most visible here, likely by Agrippa II. The temple constructed by Herod is the best candidate for the Augusteum which he built in the vicinity of Panias, the headwaters of the Jordan River, to honor Caesar Augustus.*

stored millions of gallons of water at each of these desert fortresses, plenty to not only withstand potential siege but to supply Herod's lavish pools and baths. Among the earlier buildings built at Masada was the Western Palace, similar in style to the Hasmonean palace at Jericho. The Masada palace included service and living rooms around an open square courtyard, and likely continued to be the "working" area as other structures were added to the site. Herod also erected two palaces at Jericho in this early phase of building activity, greatly enlarging the Hasmonean structures already there. These included pools and colonnaded gardens both south and north of the wadi. Also to this period likely belong the three soaring towers north of Herod's palace on the western hill of Jerusalem, named (according to Josephus; *War* 5.161–175) after Herod's brother Phasael, his friend Hippicus, and his wife Mariamme. The lower part of one of these towers (either Phasael or Hippicus) is still visible to a height of nearly seventy feet today. Also visible to its full height is the structure Herod built at Machpelah in Hebron over the traditional site of the Tombs of the Patriarchs. It was constructed with distinctive Herodian margin-and-boss ashlar masonry, with engaged pilasters on the upper half of the structure. There is fragmentary evidence that the upper courses of the wall enclosing the Temple Mount in Jerusalem were constructed the same way.

The second phase of Herod's building projects included cities and temples:

- Herod constructed three temples to Caesar Augustus, the first Roman emperor to declare himself divine. All have been excavated. One is adjacent to the harbor of Caesarea Maritima. A second was built over the remains of Ahab's palace in Samaria, a city that Herod renamed Sebaste, the Greek form of Augustus. The third has been found at Khirbet Omrit south of the Pan shrine at Banias near one of the main headwaters of the Jordan River. Each was positioned to be seen from a long distance and served to mark, as it were, the land for Rome.

- Herod founded Caresarea Maritima to provide a new, unrivaled port on the Mediterranean that had equal access to both Galilee and Judea. Excavated remains at Caesarea Maritima that can be attributed to Herod include the theater, a palace surrounding a pool on a spit of rock that juts into the Mediterranean (the "promontory palace"), and the harbor. For the harbor's breakwater, Herod's workmen introduced to the region

**CAESAREA MARITIMA**

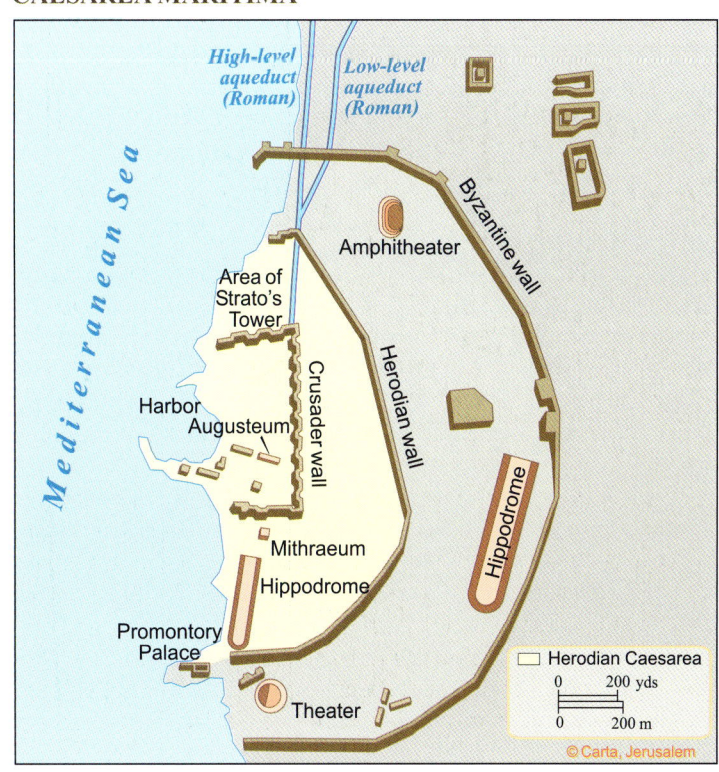

*Herod the Great used* opus reticulatum *and* opus quadratum *in constructing the bathhouse of his opulent Third Palace in Jericho. He covered the* opus *work with frescoed plaster. Herod was the first to construct circular buildings in Judea; the Frigidarium of his Jericho bathhouse, shown here, was one.*

the use of concrete that could harden underwater. The city was built on the Hippodamian plan.

- Herod built Herodium as the palace fortress closest to, and in sight of, Jerusalem, essentially as a monument to himself. Within the open-topped mountain Herod installed gardens, a dining hall and a bathhouse, with a pleasure garden and colonnaded pool at its base. Water for the facility was provided by a private aqueduct that flowed from Solomon's Pools. Recently uncovered at Herodium was a theatre built for the royal visit of Marcus Agrippa, son-in-law of Augustus, in 16 B.C. The royal room adjacent to the theatre was decorated with paintings on dry plaster, much brighter in color than were the frescoes used elsewhere. Also recently discovered at Herodium is Herod's tomb, the outer monument (*nefesh*) of which would have been visible from Jerusalem. Pieces of Herod's sarcophagus have also been recovered. Of reddish limestone, it was apparently intentionally smashed in the first century by Jews who took over Herodium in the Great Revolt.

**HERODIUM—PLAN OF THE PALACE-FORTRESS**

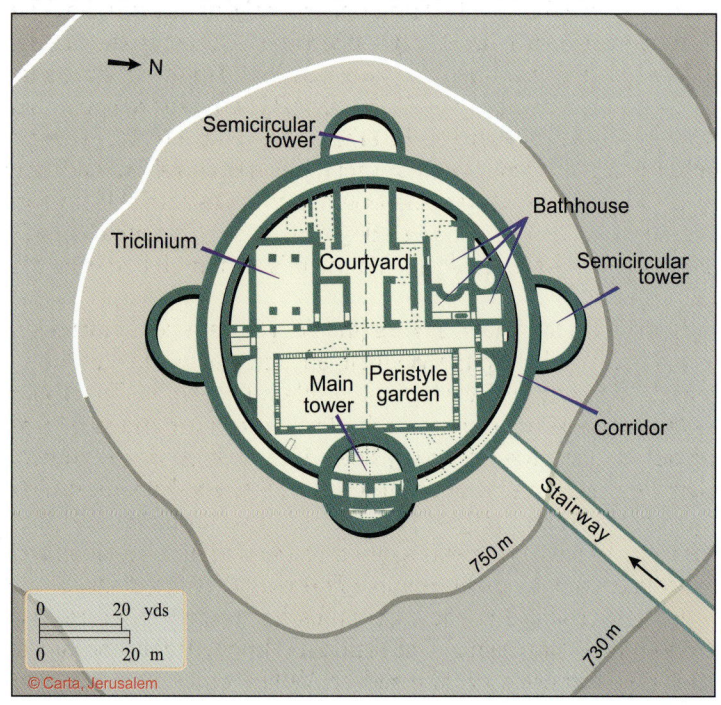

- Herod's only desert fortress east of the Rift, Machaerus, has not been well excavated. Still, there is evidence of the requisite bathhouse, mosaics, palace and peristyle court.
- Better excavated is Herod's third palace at Jericho, with wings on both the northern and southern banks of the Wadi Qelt connected by an arched bridge. The palace contained a reception hall, two peristyle courtyards with Ionic and Corinthian capitals, *opus sectile* floors, frescoed walls and a bathhouse. The walls of the palace were constructed like those built in Rome, of *opus reticulatum* (diamond-shaped stones) with *opus quadratum* (rectangular stones) for the corners, all plastered over and frescoed. Herod also used cast concrete covered with decorated stucco for ceilings and domes.
- The northern palace at Masada and its outbuildings also apparently belong to this mature phase of Herod's building projects. The palace included all of the elements of his other palaces, but placed them on the awe-inspiring, three-tiered northern point of Masada, with a one-thousand-foot drop to the ground below. Because Masada seems to have been built and destroyed within a period of less than one hundred years, all of its pottery dates to the same time span. It thus became the type-site for identifying first century pottery.
- An industrial installation at 'En Boqeq south of Qumran was used to process balsam, valued in Rome as a healing agent and perfume. A boat dock from the period has been found at 'En Boqeq and another directly across the Dead Sea at Callirrhoe, where the hot springs were noted for their recreational and therapeutic value.
- Remains of Herodian-era forts, functional though not palatial, have also been found at Arad, Beer-sheba, Aroer and Tel 'Ira in the Negev.

Most impressive, however, is what Herod planned for Jerusalem. By the time the city was destroyed by the Romans in A.D. 70, it had become a true world-class urban center, with the highest standards of the day. This can be seen in its public infrastructure and many private homes. It is difficult to know exactly how much of the work was done during Herod's own lifetime, but he certainly can be credited for setting the tone. Archaeological remains abound:

The Temple Mount was expanded to the west and south by huge retaining walls of massive stone ashlars that spanned the city's central valley. The largest ashlar is estimated to weigh 600 tons. At the northernmost end of the western wall, exposed bedrock was incorporated into the foundations of the wall by carving it to look like Herodian margin-and-boss ashlars.

Remains of a monumental stairway descended from Robinson's Arch above the southwestern corner of the Temple Mount to the level of the paved street below. The street was lined with shops, which suggests that it was an important business corridor in the city. The fresh condition of the stones that paved the street indicate that it was repaved not long before the city's destruction in A.D. 70, probably by Herod Agrippa II (*Ant.* 20.222). A stone set into the pinnacle of the southwestern corner of the Temple Mount retaining wall, found broken in excavation, bore the inscription "to the place of the trumpeting...." This must have marked the spot of announcement of Temple activities.

A monumental stairway, with adjacent *miqva'ot*, led to the Hulda Gates, the main entrance to the Temple complex on its southern side. The interior of the gates were constructed with highly decorated domes, still *in situ* underneath the Temple Mount platform though closed to public view.

Virtually nothing is left of the Royal Stoa that was built in the basilica style on the southern end of the platform above, or of the portico surrounding the platform, or of the Temple itself. A few fragmentary architectural pieces including capitals and friezes carved with intricate floral and geometric designs have been found, but it is not possible to match them with any particular part of the complex. A few fragments of colorful *opus sectile* suggest that the platform was paved in the style of the courtyards of Herod's palaces. Josephus mentions that the complex was built in the Corinthian style (*Ant.* 15.414), but most of the extant remains are of the Ionic order.

Quarries for the huge stones used in building the Temple Mount structures have been found under the Church of the Holy Sepulchre, in Jerusalem's Russian Compound northwest of the Old City, and in the Ramat Shlomo neighborhood several miles northwest of the city.

Josephus mentions a Second Wall that followed a looping course northward from somewhere east of Herod's Palace to the Antonia Fortress on the northwestern corner of the Temple Mount (*War* 5.146, 158). Its line would have left the area of the Holy Sepulchre church outside of the city. Very little of this wall has been found archaeologically except for a few courses of stone along the eastern face of the western tower of Damascus Gate. Remnants of a Third Wall (*War* 5.147–155) constructed by Agrippa I to surround a large area of extramural suburbs north of the city have also been uncovered, about 500 meters north of Damascus Gate.

The interior of Herod's Jerusalem palace was, according to Josephus (*War* 5.178), "indescribable." Little or nothing remains, but it might be compared to mansions of Jerusalem's elite that have been found in Jerusalem's Jewish Quarter. These had *miqva'ot*, mosaics, frescoed walls, and decorated stucco ceilings. A broken piece of wall plaster found in the remains of the mansion that has been incorporated into the Wohl Museum contained an etching of a menorah, likely similar in style to the golden menorah in the Temple. Artifacts found inside these mansions include beautiful stone vessels turned on lathes, stone tables and an elegant blue-green glass vase made by Ennion, a known glassblower from Sidon. Also found were vessels of Terra Sigillata Ware, both Eastern (made

## PLAN OF MASADA

in Phoenicia) and Western (from Italy). These were fine, expensive angular dishes with a high burnish and bright red slip.

More common in the city and not nearly as expensive was locally-made Jerusalem Ware. These were vessels with brown-red floral designs on their inside surfaces similar to decorations found on Nabatean pottery. A disproportionately large number of cooking pots were found around the perimeter of Jerusalem. These had probably been purchased by pilgrims, then discarded before the journey home.

The Herodian-era Pool of Siloam, surrounded by a columned portico, repaved an earlier Hasmonean pool on the same site. The entire pool seems to have been stepped so as to provide easy access to large groups of people. The pool was fed by the southern outlet of the Iron II conduit of Hezekiah's tunnel. Two stepped streets led from the pool northward to the area of the Temple Mount, one on either side of the central valley. Their paving stones show evidence of the same kind of margin-and-boss design that is seen in Herodian wall construction. A sophisticated system of underground channels carried rain wastewater from Jerusalem's western hill toward the Siloam Pool.

Remains of the Sheep's Pools (the Pool of Bethesda) have been found north of the Temple Mount in an area that would have been outside of the city wall for most of the Herodian Period. The pools, rectangular and adjacent to each other, were surrounded by five porticoes, one on each strong side with a fifth between the two. Byzantine-era remains of an Aesclepion, a Greco-Roman healing site dedicated to the god Aesclepios, were found in the pool complex. Its presence may suggest that a similar Aesclepion served the soldiers of the nearby Antonia Fortress in the first century.

Approximately 800 rock-cut tombs have been found in and around Jerusalem dating to the Herodian Period. Among the largest and most elaborate are the Kidron Valley tombs (the so-called

# JERUSALEM IN THE SECOND TEMPLE PERIOD

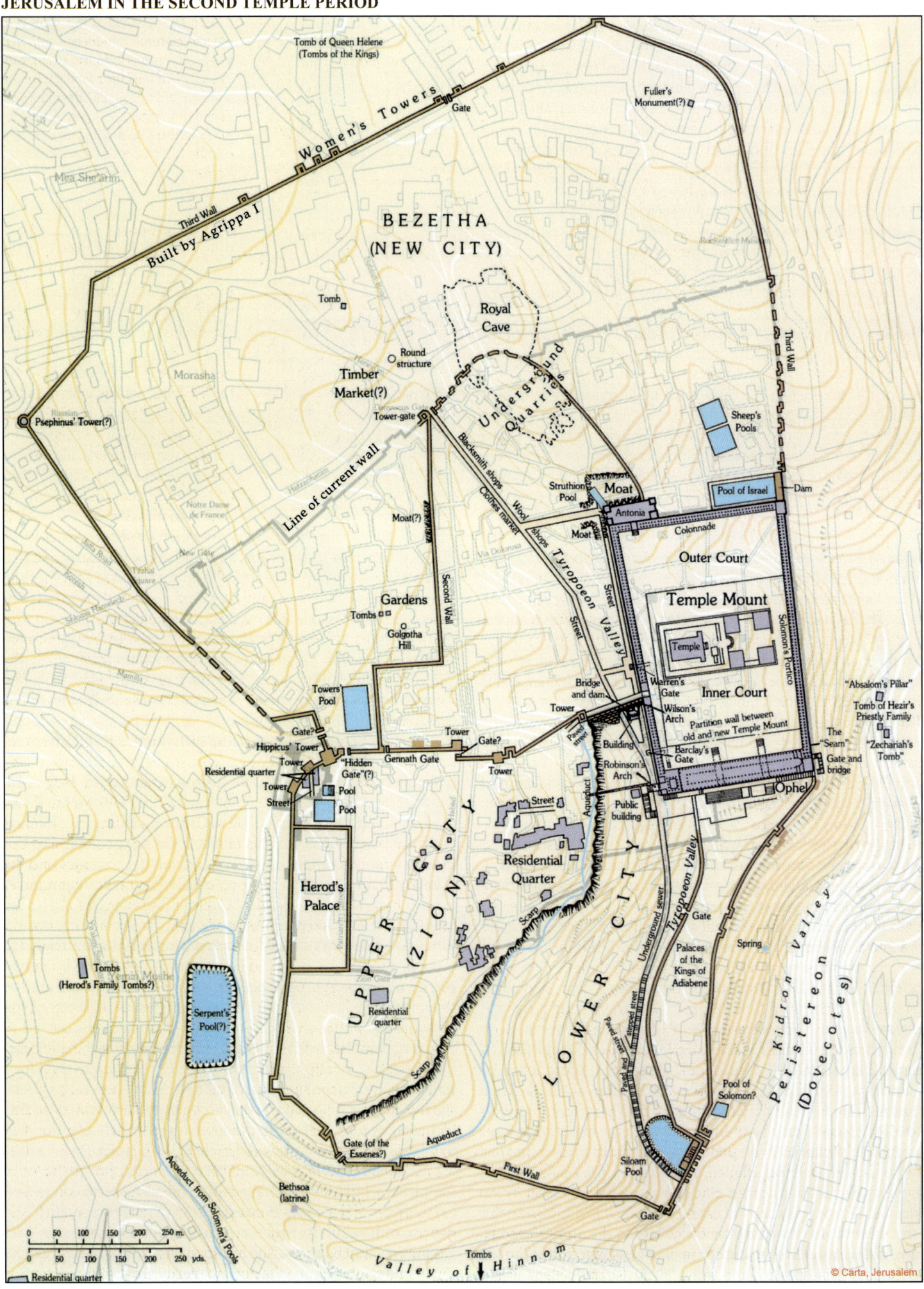

*The housing found in Jewish villages in first century Galilee were often built in the* insula *style, a conglomeration of small rooms set around shared courtyards. Each insula was home to an extended family of three to four generations. The local building material for villages around the Sea of Galilee was basalt, giving a dark but homey look to its dwellings.*

seems to have been a living center for the community who produced the Dead Sea Scrolls (the Essenes). The Hasmonean site at Qumran was rebuilt after the earthquake of 31 B.C., then destroyed by the Romans in A.D. 68. It includes an aqueduct system that filled the site's many *miqva'ot* and cisterns, workshops to produce pottery (all of which was utilitarian and non-decorated), a room for communal meals, and a room with benches and inkwells that seems to have been used to produce scrolls. Altogether thousands of pieces of over 400 scrolls have been found in eleven nearby caves. These include texts of the Hebrew Bible and texts relating specifically to the community (commentaries, rules of order and the like).

The Nabateans were also erecting structures that rivaled those of Herod the Great. Pride of place are the rock-carved façades at Petra, most of which seem to have been tombs while others were related to the devotion of local deities. As in Jerusalem, the architectural forms at Petra and other Nabatean sites in Edom, Moab and the Negev show a creative combination of Greek, Egyptian, Mesopotamian and native Nabatean forms. Nabatean pottery is some of the finest produced anywhere in the ancient world: red-orange in color and very thin with brown dots and lines decorating the interior surfaces.

Archaeological evidence for efforts related to the Great Revolt (A.D. 66–70) can be found in alterations at two of Herod's palace fortresses, where a banqueting hall at Herodium and a stable at Masada were converted into synagogues. Locally minted Jewish coins bearing inscriptions "Jerusalem the holy" also indicate a concerted effort to reestablish an independent Jewish state in the Judean hills. Evidence of Rome's response can be seen in destruction layers at sites such as Jotapata, Gamla, Qumran, Herodium, Cypros, Jerusalem and, in A.D. 73, Masada. Jericho seems to have gone out of use sometime prior. In Jerusalem, some of the most dramatic archaeological evidence for the destruction of the city is seen in the deliberate smashing of streets by the Pool of Siloam, confirming Josephus' horrifying account of Romans attacking Jews who had hidden in the sewers (*War* 6.370, 401–402, 429–430). Contra the account of Josephus, there is little archaeological evidence of Rome's campaigns in Perea, Idumea and on the coast.

Rome's subsequent takeover of Judea is also apparent in the archaeological record. Stones and clay tiles bearing the inscription LEG X FRET (Legio X Fretensis) indicate that the Tenth Roman legion camped on the ruined site of Herod's palace. Flavius Silva, the general who captured Masada, erected an honorific arch on the Temple Mount, fragmentary remains of which can still be seen in the Islamic Museum on the site. Coins, too, tell the story: the Roman takeover was honored by a special mint of Judaea Capta coins depicting Judea as a woman slumped beneath a palm.

Now that the southern Levant was officially Roman, many sites grew dramatically. Most of the archaeological evidence of growth in the Decapolis and other Greco-Roman cities of the region can be dated to the reigns of Trajan (98–117) and Hadrian (117–138) who sought to incorporate this southeastern bend of the Mediterranean into their empire by active building campaigns. Hadrian's visit to the region in A.D. 128–130 prompted a spurt of monumental building activity, including triple-arched gates in Jerusalem and Gerasa (Jerash).

Some archaeological evidence confirms the Bar Kochba revolt of A.D. 132–135. Though little has been found in Jerusalem, Jewish coins bearing the inscription "year 1 (and year 2) of the redemption of Israel" are indication enough. One Bar Kochba coin depicts a building that must have been the Jerusalem Temple in all of its pre-destruction, Herodian-style glory. Caves and tunnels hewn at Herodium and at Ḥorvat Midras and Ḥorvat 'Itri in the mid-Shephelah attest to what was, quite literally, an underground struggle for independence. Caches of skeletons, as well as routine documents such as wills and marriage contracts, have been found in caves above En-gedi. These offer ready testimony to the realities of everyday life under siege during the last days of the failed revolt.

*Remains of several small household* miqva'ot *can be seen at Jotapata, the city that was the last stand of the Jewish forces in Galilee during the Great Revolt. Artifactual evidence such as these serve as good indicators of the ethnicity of the population of a city in ancient times.*

*Two monumental tombs in Jerusalem's Kidron Valley attest to the ways that diverse cultural influences combined into unique forms in Herod's kingdom. The tomb of the Hezir family is on the left; a tomb traditionally identified with Zechariah is on the right. Elements of the Doric and Ionic orders are combined with Egyptian and Nabatean forms in their façades.*

Absalom's Pillar and Tomb of Zechariah). These combined Greek, Egyptian and Nabatean architectural forms. Also of note are the tomb of the Nazarite and the tomb of Nicanor, the later a benefactor of the Temple, on the northern end of the Mount of Olives. Others include the Tombs of the Kings directly north of the city, the tombs of Sanhedriya to the northwest, the so-called Herod's Family tomb west of the city and the Akeldama Tomb at the confluence of the Hinnom and Kidron valleys to the south. Elaborate tombs of the period were typically cut out of natural cliffs or rock faces exposed by quarrying. Their architectural elements included an open-air forecourt with an adjacent monument (*nefesh*) leading to an inner vestibule off of which were burial chambers. These chambers were either *kochim* (long, narrow openings into which the body was laid end-wise) or *arcosolia*, horizontal benches crowned by an arch. Many had highly decorated exterior entrances, sometimes sized to resemble doorways of palaces. Some interior ceilings were decorated in palatial styles. Very few rolling stone tombs have been found in and around Jerusalem; one is at the so-called Herod's Family tomb; another is the Tombs of the Kings (both are names of tradition). A third can be seen at Ḥorvat Midras in the central Shephelah, while a fourth is just west of Mishmar Ha'Emeq on the southern edge of the Jezreel Valley.

Herod the Great largely neglected Galilee in his building efforts. His son Antipas made up for the gap, with ambitious projects at both Sepphoris and Tiberias. Sepphoris was rebuilt as "the ornament of all Galilee" (*Ant.* 18.27) following its destruction by the Romans who suppressed a local revolt there at the death of Herod the Great. Yet the archaeological data is not clear to what extent the classic Greco-Roman character that came to dominate the city in the Late Roman Period was already in place in the first century. The theater, for instance, which is typically one of the first structures erected in a Roman city, seems to have been built only in the late first or early second century A.D. One positive indicator as to the local, Jewish character of the city in the early Herodian Period is that over fifty percent of the kitchenware found at the site was made at Kfar Hananya, a small (likely Jewish) village fifteen miles northeast. This suggests that people from surrounding villages benefited economically through sales, employment or trade with larger centers such as Sepphoris, whether these centers looked Roman, Jewish or a little of both. Archaeological evidence for Tiberias, which was founded as the new capital of Galilee in A.D. 17 (*Ant.* 18.36–38), reveals a gate, towers and roads, all made of basalt, though most of the ancient city still lies under the modern city of the same name.

Herod's son Philip the Tetrarch founded two cities as *polis*, Bethsaida on the northeastern plain of the Sea of Galilee and Caesarea Philippi at Banias (*Ant.* 18.28). The archaeological remains of Bethsaida which date to the first century A.D. consist of a few *insula* housing units with no evidence of larger structures that typically identify a site as being Roman. At Banias, however, there are extensive remains typical of a *polis*, including an expansive palace, streets and a sophisticated water system. Some of these elements were constructed by Philip, others by Agrippa II.

Many of the sites which have been excavated in Galilee attest to the region's Jewish character. These are concentrated on the northwestern shore of the Sea of Galilee (Capernaum, Bethsaida, Chorazin and Magdala), and in the area of the Beth Netofa Valley in western Galilee (Nazareth, Khirbet Qanah and Jotapata). Markers of Jewish ethnicity that can be found in the archaeological record include *miqva'ot*, stone vessels, *kokhim* tombs, ossuaries and the absence of pork bones. The same indicators are also common at sites in Judea. Typical as well of Galilee villages are *insula*, walled housing units enclosing a mix of small interior rooms and courtyards. Remains at Nazareth dating to the first century A.D. are meager (oil presses, granaries, cisterns, wells, etc.) and indicate only that the place was a small agricultural village, certainly typical of many other sites in the region. There are no remains of a first century synagogue in Nazareth, although such a building has been uncovered at Magdala, complete with a large squared stone depicting a menorah. The basalt foundation under the Late Roman white limestone synagogue at Capernaum may well date to the first century. The site of Khirbet es-Salam on the lower slopes of the Golan, popularly identified as Gamla,[65] preserves excavated remains of a fortified town replete with living spaces typical of Jewish villages as well as a synagogue. One must add that the coins and pottery types of Galilee sites indicate that the region also had a strong connection to Phoenicia, a reality that makes sense on economic (market) and geographical grounds though not on religious criteria.

Qumran must be considered a unique site. This walled compound on an arid terrace above the northwestern corner of the Dead Sea

*Roof tile stamped with the emblem of the Tenth Roman Legion, found in Jerusalem.*

*(below) Coin of Judaea Capta. The image on the right is Vespasian; that on the left depicts a captive Jewish woman in mourning next to an emblem of victory. The word Judaea is below. Because coins traveled widely, they announced Rome's authority across the empire. (Reuben and Edith Hecht Museum, Haifa Univ.)*

**Biblical Connections.** As might be expected, an archaeological record as rich and varied for the southern Levant as is that of the Early Roman Period has clear and important points of contact with the New Testament. The opportunities as well as the challenges that the heavy Greco-Roman presence in the land offered the residents of Judea, Samaria and Galilee provide an overall cultural backdrop for the texts and events of the Gospels. Similarly, evidences of a varied Jewish presence speak of a full-bodied religious-national identity that infused the region with alternate views of the good life.

Regarding the accounts of the Gospels, with rare exception nothing should be expected to be found archaeologically that can be related with confidence to specific events in the life of Jesus. On the other hand, much is contextual, though much is seen only through the lenses of early Church tradition. Neither Bethlehem nor Nazareth of the first century were the kind of village that left archaeologists data beyond what could be termed the nondescript material culture of everyday life. Sepphoris provides more, though it, too, seems to have been comfortably Jewish and only emergently Greco-Roman during Jesus' formative years. Still, the city was a lively urban center in which Jesus could have not only practiced his skills as a *tekton* (a skilled workman in local building materials; cf. Mt 13:55; Mk 6:3), but been exposed to a colorful matrix of Galilee life. Though the Gospels never mention that Jesus ever went to any of the Romanized urban centers of the area, including Sepphoris or Tiberias, it was cities such as these that made the Beth Netofa Valley and the Sea of Galilee international arenas in his day. It is important to note that the focus of Jesus' activity took place in precisely the two areas in Galilee where most of the ethnic markers designating a strong Jewish presence can be found in the archaeological record prior to A.D. 70, and that there is material evidence of a Roman presence penetrating exactly these same areas at the same time.

All sorts of small artifacts common to Galilee illustrate statements made by Jesus, especially in his parables, or serve as "stage props" for events described in the Gospels. These include sheep pens, oil lamps, *insula* houses, mill stones and the like. One of the *insula* in Capernaum, just south of the basalt foundation remains of the town's synagogue (Lk 7:5), preserves remnant remains of a house-church in the late first century A.D. In the mid-fifth century, a large octagon church was built over the site, confirming in stone the memory that this particular *insula* was the home of Peter. A number of harbors, quays and piers, together with boat anchors and fishing net weights, have been found around the Sea of Galilee, the highest concentration of which were on the northern shore of the lake (especially at Capernaum). The hull of a single-mast sailboat from the first century, the kind that would have carried fishermen, has been found off the shore of Magdala. All of these provide a package of material that illustrates the stories of the Gospels.

On the upper end of the socio-economic scale, the stone storage jars found in homes of the elite from Jerusalem must have been similar to those present at the wedding in Cana (Jn 2:6). Excavations at Khirbet Qanah show the town to have been prosperous, a Jewish counterpoint to the city of Sepphoris on the opposite side of the Beth Netofa Valley. Jesus' first public appearance, then, was in a home that seems to have had more in common with the cultural horizon of Jerusalem than with the bulk of the villages of Galilee. The lack of synagogue buildings in Galilee from the first century may suggest that synagogue meetings in the poorer villages took place in locations other than at designated buildings, such as in public areas out of doors, in courtyards or in private homes. This reconstruction reminds us of the kind of outdoor locations where the Apostle Paul sometimes met Jewish congregations in the Diaspora (Acts 16:13).

It is in Jerusalem where the footprint of first century A.D. material culture is the most impressive, and there are clear referents to parts of the city's infrastructure in the Gospels. The Pinnacle of the Temple (Mt 4:5), the Temple portico (Jn 10:23) and the pools of Bethesda (Jn 5:2) and Siloam (Jn 9:7) all provide a nice juxtaposition of archaeology and text. So does the inscription found in secondary use at Caesarea which mentions Pontius Pilate, Rome's representative in Jerusalem at the time of Jesus' trial, by both name and title (Prefect of Judea). The stairway leading up to the Temple Mount from the south, though not mentioned in the Gospels, provides a likely setting for Jesus' final discourse (Mt 23:1–39) because nearly all of the physical images he used in his sermon could have been seen from the stairs. The architectural layout of the palatial mansion now incorporated into the Wohl Museum in the Jewish Quarter fits nicely the flow of the narrative of Peter's denial of Jesus in the home of Caiaphas. While there is no necessary reason to think that this particular home belonged to the high priest, archaeologists have uncovered Caiaphas' "eternal home," that is, his ossuary, a highly decorated limestone box inscribed with his name. An ossuary found in a tomb at Givat ha-Mivtar north of the Old City of Jerusalem contained the remains of a crucified man—the heal bone was pierced by a nail, still *in situ*. From this it is possible to reconstruct details about the raw physicality of crucifixion. The elaborate tombs surrounding Jerusalem in the first century give indication of the nature of the family tomb of Joseph of Arimathea, a prominent member of the Jewish ruling aristocracy (Mk 15:43), into which the body of Jesus was laid.

Other sites venerated as places where Jesus was are largely sites of tradition, hallowed by the collective memory of the Church over the ages. All carry an archaeological witness, most of which dates to the centuries following the close of the Gospel story. It is sites like these that tell us much about the way that material culture preserved the priorities of the Church from century to century, but this opens another chapter in the intersection of text and artifact. To the extent that such sites draw the visitor into the worlds of the New and Old Testaments, they, too, remain an important part of biblical archaeology.

# Notes and References

1. The Koran, post-dating the Roman Empire, is more recent.
2. Of the many helpful articles on the subject see for instance Ann Killebrew, "Between Heaven and Earth: Educational Perspectives on the Archaeology and Material Culture of the Bible," in *Between Text and Artifact: Integrating Archaeology in Biblical Studies Teaching*, ed. Milton C. Moreland (Atlanta: SBL, 2003), 11–30.
3. For a survey of early exploration in the southern Levant see Yehoshua Ben-Arieh, *The Rediscovery of the Holy Land in the Nineteenth Century* (Jerusalem: Magnes, 1979).
4. Flinders Petrie, *Seventy Years in Archaeology* (London: Sampson Low, Marston, 1931), 113–118; J. Garrow Duncan, *Corpus of Dated Palestine Pottery* (London: British School of Archaeology in Egypt, 1930).
5. Note the analysis of Neil Asher Silberman, *Digging for God and Country: Exploration in the Holy Land, 1799–1917* (New York: Doubleday, 1982).
6. See for instance Albright's great synthesis of archaeological, historical and theological thought, *From Stone Age to Christianity: Monotheism and the Historical Process* (Baltimore: Johns Hopkins, 1940); as well as his *The Archaeology of Palestine* (Gloucester, MA: Peter Smith, 1971) and G. Ernest Wright, *Biblical Archaeology*, new and rev. ed., (Philadelphia: Westminster, 1962).
7. It still is, though by being housed in a branch of the national government (the Israel Antiquities Authority), in the autonomous Israel Exploration Society and in separate academic departments in the Israeli university system, archaeology in Israel nowadays very much fosters independent tracks of inquiry.
8. Kathleen M. Kenyon, *Beginning in Archaeology*, rev. ed. (New York: Praeger, 1957). Though a bit dated, a base-line introduction to field excavation techniques remains William G. Dever and H. Darrell Lance, eds. *A Manual of Field Excavation: Handbook for Field Archaeologists* (Cincinnati: Hebrew Union College-Jewish Institute of Religion, 1978).
9. As examples see William G. Dever, "Impact of the 'New Archaeology,'" in *Benchmarks in Time and Culture: An Introduction to Palestinian Archaeology Dedicated to Joseph A. Callaway*, ed. Joel F. Drinkard, Jr., Gerald L. Mattingly and J. Maxwell Miller (Atlanta: Scholars Press, 1988), 337–352; Walter Rast, *Through the Ages in Palestinian Archaeology: An Introductory Handbook* (Philadelphia: Trinity Press International, 1992) and Volkmar Fritz, *An Introduction to Biblical Archaeology*, JSOTSup 172 (Sheffield: JSOT, 1994).
10. Note the state of affairs as described by Anson Rainey, "Stones for Bread: Archaeology Versus History," *Near Eastern Archaeology* 64/3 (2001): 140–149.
11. The debate is perhaps best illustrated by in the change in name of *The Biblical Archaeologist*, the scholarly journal founded by G. Ernest Wright back in 1938, to *Near Eastern Archaeology* in 1998, and the much larger readership of the journal *Biblical Archaeology Review* (started in 1975) which in many ways has co-opted the general market in preserving the more traditional biblical archaeology name.
12. Recent examples are Philip J. King and Lawrence E. Stager, *Life in Biblical Israel* (Louisville: Westminster John Knox, 2001); Andrew G. Vaughn and Ann E. Killebrew, eds., *Jerusalem in Bible and Archaeology: The First Temple Period* (Atlanta: Society of Biblical Literature, 2003) and even the works of William G. Dever such as *What Did the Biblical Writers Know & When Did They Know It? What Archaeology Can Tell Us about the Reality of Ancient Israel* (Grand Rapids: Eerdmans, 2001).
13. Dever, *What Did the Biblical Writers Know & When Did They Know It*, 89.
14. John M. Monson, "Enter Joshua: The 'Mother of Current Debates' in Biblical Archaeology," in *Do Historical Matters Matter to Faith? A Critical Appraisal of Modern and Postmodern Approaches to Scripture*, ed. James K. Hoffmeier and Dennis R. Magary (Wheaton: Crossway, 2012), 439.
15. Anson F. Rainey and R. Steven Notley, *The Sacred Bridge* (Jerusalem: Carta, 2006), 24. Note the similar assessment of the epigrapher Joseph Naveh quoted in Shaul Shaked, "Obituary for Joseph Naveh," *IEJ* 62/1 (2012): 113.
16. Anson Rainey, "Stones for Bread: Archaeology versus History," *Near East Archaeology* 64/3 (2001): 140.
17. For example, Nahman Avigad, *Hebrew Bullae from the Time of Jeremiah: Remnants of a Burnt Archive* (Jerusalem: IES, 1986).
18. From the time of the Israelite monarchy see for instance Shmuel Aḥituv, *Echoes from the Past: Hebrew and Cognate Inscriptions from the Biblical Period* (Jerusalem: Carta, 2008); and Wayne Horowitz and Takayoshi Oshima, *Cuneiform in Canaan: Cuneiform Sources from the Land of Israel in Ancient Times* (Jerusalem: IES, 2006). Best known of many texts from the time of the New Testament found by archaeologists are those from Qumran; Michael Wise, Martin Abegg, Jr., & Edward Cook, *The Dead Sea Scrolls: A New Translation* (New York: HarperCollins, 1996).
19. K. A. Kitchen, *On the Reliability of the Old Testament* (Grand Rapids: Eerdmans, 2003), 449–500.
20. Andrew E. Vaughn, "Is Biblical Archaeology Theologically Useful Today? Yes, A Programmatic Proposal," in Vaughn and Killebrew, *Jerusalem in Bible and Archaeology*, 407–430.
21. Aharoni, *The Archaeology of the Land of Israel*, transl. by Anson F. Rainey (Philadelphia: Westminster, 1978).
22. James B. Pritchard, ed., *Ancient Near Eastern Texts Relating to the Old Testament* (*ANET*) (Princeton: Princeton University Press, 1955), 228.
23. Suzanne Richard, "Toward a Consensus of Opinion on the End of the Early Bronze Age in Palestine-Transjordan," *BASOR* 237 (1980): 5–34.
24. See the summary in Mazar, *Archaeology of the Land of the Bible*, 169–171; and Ram Gophna, "The Intermediate Bronze Age" in Amnon Ben-Tor, ed., *The Archaeology of Ancient Israel*, transl. by R. Greenberg (New Haven: Yale, 1992), 156–158.
25. Mazar, *Archaeology of the Land of the Bible*, 152.
26. See Mazar, *Archaeology of the Land of the Bible*, 188 for a short discussion.
27. Rainey and Notley, *The Sacred Bridge*, 58.
28. Rainey and Notley, *The Sacred Bridge*, 56–57.
29. Horowitz and Oshima, *Cuneiform in Canaan*, and Wayne Horowitz, Takayoshi Oshima and Filip Vukosavović, "Haxor 18: Fragments of a Cuneiform Law Collection from Hazor," *IEJ* 62 (2012): 1548–176.
30. Rainey and Notley, *The Sacred Bridge*, 59.
31. Mazar 231, note 61.
32. Note also the evidence Semites moving peacefully into Egypt during MB as shown on the tomb paintings at Beni Hasan in Upper Egypt; see Barry J. Kemp, *Ancient Egypt: Anatomy of a Civilization* (London: Routledge, 1989), 246–248.
33. Kitchen, *On the Reliability of the Old Testament*, 318–338.
34. To borrow a title from Kenneth A. Kitchen, *Pharaoh Triumphant: The Life and Times of Rameses II, King of Egypt* (Warminster: Aris & Phillips, 1982).
35. William Moran, *The Amarna Letters* (Baltimore: Johns Hopkins, 1992).
36. Ronny Reich, *Excavating the City of David: Where Jerusalem's History Began* (Jerusalem: Israel Exploration Society, 2011), 288.
37. Peter van der Veen, "When Pharaohs Ruled Jerusalem," *BAR* 39/2 (2013): 42–48, 67; Eilat Mazar, Wayne Horowitz, Takayoshi Oshima and Yuval Goren, "A Cuneiform Tablet from the Ophel in Jerusalem," *IEJ* 60 (2010): 4–21.
38. *ANET*, 236.
39. *ANET*, 262–263.
40. Avraham Faust, *Israel's Ethnogenesis: Settlement, Interaction, Expansion and Resistance* (London: Equinox, 2006), 159–169, 227–228.
41. Donald B. Redford, *Akhenaten, the Heretic King* (Princeton: University Press, 1984); and Cyril Aldred, *Akhenaten, King of Egypt* (London: Thames & Hudson, 1988).
42. Monson, "Enter Joshua: The 'Mother of Current Debates' in Biblical Archaeology," in *Do Historical Matters Matter to Faith?*, 427–457.
43. Rainey and Notley, *The Sacred Bridge*, 103.
44. Anson F. Rainey, "Whence Came the Israelites and Their Language?" *IEJ* 57 (2007): 41–64.
45. Faust, *Israel's Ethnogenesis*, 35–49.
46. Aḥituv, *Echoes from the Past*; Ron Tappy and P. Kyle McCarter, Jr., eds., *Literate Culture and Tenth-Century Canaan: The Tel Zayit Abecedary in Context* (Winona Lake: Eisenbrauns, 2008).
47. For a summary of the debate with bibliography see Steven M. Ortiz, "The Archaeology of David and Solomon: Method or Madness?" in *Do Historical Matters Matter to Faith?*, 497–516.
48. Faust, *Ethnogenesis*, 111–134; and "Abandonment, Urbanization, Resettlement and the Formation of the Israelite State," *NEA* 66:3 (2003):147–161.
49. Eilat Mazar, *Discovering the Solomonic Wall in Jerusalem* (Jerusalem: Shoham, 2011).
50. Jane Cahill, "Jerusalem at the Time of the United Monarchy: The Archaeological Evidence," in *Jerusalem in the Bible and Archaeology*, eds. Andrew G. Vaughn and Anne E. Killebrew (Atlanta: SBL, 2003), 13–80.
51. James F. Osborne, "Communicating Power in the Bīt-Ḥilāni Palace," *BASOR* 368 (2012): 29–66.
52. Eilat Mazar, *The Palace of King David: Excavations at the Summit of the City of David* (Jerusalem: Shoham, 2009); contra Ronny Reich, *Excavating the City of David: Where Jerusalem's History Began* (Jerusalem: IES, 2011), 265–268.
53. *ANET*, 288.
54. John Monson, *The Architecture of Solomon's Temple* (Oxford: Oxford University, 2008).
55. Michael Hasel, "New Excavations at Khirbet Qeiyafa and the Early History of Judah," in *Do Historical Matters Matter to Faith?* 477–496; and Yigal Levin, "The Identification of Khirbet Qeiyafa: A New Suggestion," *BASOR* 367 (2012): 73–86.
56. For discussion, see Oded Lipschits, *The Fall and Rise of Jerusalem: Judah Under Babylonian Rule* (Winona Lake, IN: Eisenbrauns, 2005), 185–271.
57. Lipschits, *The Fall and Rise of Jerusalem*, 160–161.
58. Ritmeyer takes a more optimistic view of the archaeological evidence for Nehemiah's wall. Leen and Kathleen Ritmeyer, *Jerusalem in the Time of Nehemiah* (Jerusalem: Carta, 2005).
59. Ran Zadok, *The Jews in Babylonia during the Chaldean and Achaemenian Periods* (Haifa: University of Haifa Press, 1979).
60. *ANET*, 491–491; S. G. Rosenberg, "The Jewish Temple at Elephantine," *NEA* 67 (2004): 4–13.
61. *ANET*, 315–316.
62. The reference is by Diodorus of Sicily, writing in the late first century B.C. though citing as his source Hieronymus of Cardia, an officer of Alexander the Great. Diodorus 2.48.1; 19.94.2-10.
63. Similarly, a casual visitor to any of the sites in Israel or Jordan today that have imposing Roman-style architecture, such as Scythopolis, Gedara or Jerash, is tempted to equate the look of the site with the Early Roman Period, even though the bulk of the reconstructed remains date to the time of the earthquake of A.D. 749, long after both the Roman and Byzantine Periods ended in the region.
64. Peter Richardson, *Herod* (Columbia: University of South Carolina, 1996), 197–202.
65. On the strength of the preservation of toponyms (place names), Khirbet es-Salam is probably ancient Solyma (Josephus, *Life*, 187) whereas Gamla should be sought at Tell el-Ahdab near the village of Jamleh in the Ruqqad branch of the Yarmuk River in Syria. Satellite pictures of Tell el-Ahdab match the description of Gamla given by Josephus (*War* 4.5–8) as well as they do Khirbet es-Salam.